BLOOD, SWEAT,
AND FEAR

BLOOD
SWEAT
AND
FEAR

EVE LAZARUS

ARSENAL PULP PRESS
VANCOUVER

ARSENAL PULP PRESS
Suite 202 – 211 East Georgia St.
Vancouver, BC V6A 1Z6
Canada
arsenalpulp.com

The publisher gratefully acknowledges the support of the Canada Council for the Arts and the British Columbia Arts Council for its publishing program, and the Government of Canada (through the Canada Book Fund) and the Government of British Columbia (through the Book Publishing Tax Credit Program) for its publishing activities.

Cover and text design by Oliver McPartlin
Edited by Susan Safyan
Cover image adapted from a photo by James Crookall, Vancouver Archives reference number AM640-S1-: CVA 260-617

Printed and bound in Canada

Library and Archives Canada Cataloguing in Publication:
Lazarus, Eve, author
     Blood, sweat, and fear : the story of Inspector Vance, Vancouver's first forensic investigator / Eve Lazarus.

Issued in print and electronic formats.
ISBN 978-1-55152-685-0 (softcover).--ISBN 978-1-55152-686-7 (HTML)

     1. Vance, John F. C. B., 1884-1964. 2. Forensic scientists--British Columbia--Vancouver--Biography. 3. Forensic sciences--British Columbia--Vancouver--History. 4. Criminal investigation--British Columbia--Vancouver--History. 5. Vancouver (B.C.)--Biography. I. Title.

HV8073.L29 2017   363.25092   C2017-901405-6
                                            C2017-901406-4

For Mike, Mark, Megan, and Matthew
and for
Marian Susannah (Vance) Pocock

CONTENTS

INTRODUCTION

I first "met" Inspector John F.C.B. Vance when I was writing my book *Cold Case Vancouver*. He turned up at a crime scene in Chapter 1, the murder of Jennie Eldon Conroy, a twenty-four-year-old war worker who was beaten to death and dumped at the West Vancouver Cemetery. It turned out that Vance wasn't a police officer but ran the Police Bureau of Science for the Vancouver Police Department, and his cutting-edge work in forensics solved some of the most sensational cases in the first half of the last century. Unfortunately, Jennie's wasn't one of them.

Vance worked for most of his career out of 240 East Cordova Street, the building that now houses the Vancouver Police Museum. His daughter Marian Pocock donated his newspaper clippings, books, and photographs to the museum, and I was intrigued by this man whom the international media called the "Sherlock Holmes of Canada." I soon found out that in one year alone, seven attempts against his life were made by criminals afraid to go up against his science in the courtroom.

I needed to find out more about him and was able to track down Marian's daughter Janey Johnson who loaned me her mother's scrapbook filled with clippings about Vance. Some were neatly pasted in, others just folded, as if at some point she became overwhelmed by the sheer number of articles that featured her father. There were also some intriguing black-and-white photographs of a Model B Ford crashed into a tree and shots of detectives searching through rural buildings that I later tied to a 1934 murder of two police officers in Merritt, BC (see Chapter 7).

Janey and David Vance, another grandchild, remembered that J.F.C.B.—as Vance was known in the family—had packed up several cardboard boxes full of photographs, clippings, and case notes. No one had seen them for years, and it was thought that they'd been thrown out. And then, in July 2016, more than half a century after Vance's death, the boxes miraculously turned up in another grandchild's garage on Gabriola Island.

Incredibly, when Janey opened the first box she found a large, tattered envelope labelled *Jennie Eldon Conroy murdered West Vancouver, Dec 28, 1944*. Inside there were smaller envelopes marked with the Vancouver Police Department (VPD) insignia and filled with hair and gravel samples from the crime scene, an autopsy report, crime scene photos, and several newspaper clippings. Jennie's was one of several cases that had especially captured the inspector's imagination. He felt the evidence was important enough for him to take home with him when he retired in 1949, and then he packed it up and took it with him again years later, when he moved house. It seemed to be a sign that I should write about Vance, that we shared a fascination for this long-forgotten cold case.

When Vance started as city analyst in 1907, his work primarily consisted of ensuring that the milk, food, and municipal water supply were fit for human consumption. Forensics was still in its infancy and involved mostly toxicology and rudimentary blood work. Toxicology was essential because poison was a frequent cause of death either through choice, accident, or murder, and blood analysis was now possible after Karl Landsteiner discovered the first blood types (A, B, and O) in 1901. (A fourth type, AB, was identified the following year.) The ABO blood group system was a huge breakthrough. Now scientists could determine if a stain was blood as opposed to, say, red ink or ketchup; they could confirm whether it was human or animal, and they could then classify the specimen into one of the four blood groups. In many criminal cases, investigators could now eliminate suspects through their blood type.

Vance's first work in a police investigation involved a missing persons case in 1914. From then on, more of Vance's work involved police investigations, and by the end of 1917 almost half his time was spent solving crime. In those early years, Vancouver was the only police department in Canada that had a forensic scientist on staff and one of the few police departments in North America to use forensics.

Vance may have been paid by the police department, but he worked for the evidence, whether that convicted the guilty or set the innocent free.

Blood, Sweat, and Fear is not a biography; rather, it's the story of Vance's extraordinary work in forensic science in the first half of the last century, and in a sense, a history of the early work in forensics. Vance's job, though based in Vancouver, took him all around the province and up into the Yukon in what is one of the most interesting periods in British Columbia's history. Vance started work for the city of Vancouver four months before anti-Asian riots swept through the city. He worked through the crime-ridden Depression and two world wars, and he was employed by two of the most corrupt police chiefs in the history of the Vancouver Police Department.

Over the course of more than four decades, Vance kept his moral compass intact. During that time, he was on the forefront of forensics, often inventing his own equipment when none was available, yet today "Canada's Sherlock Holmes" is all but forgotten. My hope is that this book will change that and give John F.C.B. Vance his rightful place in the turbulent history of Vancouver.

BL00D

Tuesday, March 31, 1914

Charles Millard told his wife Clara that he'd be away for a night or two and then left his house in Vancouver's West End to catch the night ferry to Victoria. The forty-one-year-old chief ticket agent for the Canadian Pacific Railway was to meet the *S.S. Makura*, a passenger/cargo ship inbound from Australia.

The Millards did not have children, but like many households in Vancouver, they had a live-in Chinese houseboy. Kong Yew Chung, known as Yew Kong at school and Jack everywhere else, had joined them in 1910, after his father Yick Kong had scraped together the $500 Head Tax to bring him out from China. Jack stayed with his father in Mission until he was thirteen, and then he went to live with the Millards in July 1911. When he wasn't chopping wood, stoking and cleaning the furnace, cleaning house, cooking and serving meals, and washing dishes, he attended Lord Roberts Elementary School. Charles Millard told Yick Kong that because Jack was a student, he would try to have the exorbitant Head Tax refunded.

The Millards had married in 1906 and moved into their house on Pendrell Street in the West End. When the *Vancouver Elite Directory* was published two years later, eighty-six percent of the city's finest had a West End address. But in the years just before World War I, middle-class people began to move in, industry crept closer, and apartment buildings started to obstruct the view. The wealthy fled the West End for the curving boulevards and huge properties of Shaughnessy Heights, leaving their cast-off homes to become apartments and rooming houses. By

Lord Roberts Elementary in Vancouver's West End. *Eve Lazarus photo, 2017*

1914, out of the almost 2,500 people who made the Social Register that year, less than half lived in the West End.

Charles called the house at 9:00 the following evening to tell Clara that he'd be home soon, but there was no answer. When he returned home less than two hours later, Clara still wasn't home, and Jack had gone to bed. Charles went into the breakfast room, sat down, and took off his boots. He noticed that the table had been set for two and that a portion of the carpet had been scrubbed and was still damp. He was careful not to step in it. Charles phoned Clara's mother, Rachel Olmstead, in North Vancouver to see if Clara was there. She wasn't, but Charles supposed she must have gone to stay with one of her sisters, which she often did when he was away. He went to bed.

When Charles questioned Jack the next morning, the boy said that Mrs Millard had left the house around 10:30 the previous morning, but she hadn't said where she was going. She told him to stay home from school and clean, he said. Charles wasn't happy about that, but it didn't surprise him. His wife, he told people, was a "demon for cleaning." Jack asked Charles to write him a note excusing him from school, which he did.

Jack went about his duties and prepared breakfast for Charles, who then went to work. He phoned his in-laws trying to find Clara and was surprised to discover that no one had heard from her. Charles became increasingly worried. Just ten days earlier, their house had been burgled and hundreds of dollars worth of jewellery, some cash, and Clara's savings bank book had been stolen. The burglar had not been caught.

Charles came back to the house and was surprised to find that Jack had not gone to school but was down in the basement tending to a roaring fire in the furnace. Jack told him it was to heat the water to wash clothes, and Charles could see that there were already a number of things hanging on the line, including the rug from the dining room, a tablecloth, two door mats, and some towels. Jack said he hadn't gone to school because he had washed his new trousers and didn't want to wear his old ones.

Charles was bothered by the way that Jack was following him around as he moved about the house and sent him off to school in his old trousers. He then called Clara's brother Bud Olmstead to come over and help search the house to see if they could find something that would explain her whereabouts. The two men started in the attic. Aside from Jack's room in the front, there were two other rooms used as storage and a small door at the top of the staircase that led to an unfinished crawl space under the eaves. In the crawl space, they found a purple plume from Clara's hat and a veil that she normally wore when she went out, both hidden under a ledge in the eaves.

Charles called police. Detectives Albert Tisdale and James Ellice arrived at the house a little after 3:00 p.m. They questioned Charles and then went door-to-door questioning the neighbours. There were no signs of a struggle inside—at least nothing seemed out of place. Margaret Wallace, whose house looked out onto the back of the Millards', told police that she'd been working in her kitchen the morning prior and noticed a lot of smoke emanating from the chimney. Later, she told them, she saw Jack walking down the alley toward English Bay with a parcel tucked under his arm.

The detectives came back inside and looked around the breakfast room and at the wet stains on the carpet. When Detective Tisdale lifted up the carpet he found thick felt paper, which was also wet and stained. Jack was summoned, and he told the officers that he thought Clara had spilled cocoa or coffee and had tried to clean it up. The detectives thought it looked more like blood. They called their boss, Inspector John Jackson.

Jackson and Deputy Chief William McRae arrived at the house a little before 8:00 p.m. After questioning Charles and his brother-in-law, Jackson stayed to question Jack while McRae did a more thorough search of the unfinished section of the attic. There he found a pair of gloves, a coat, a skirt rolled around a hat, shoes, and a silver purse with the initials C. M.

McRae asked Charles how Jack got along with Clara. Charles told him that he was a model houseboy until recently when he started going to Chinatown on weekends and sometimes stayed away until the early hours of the morning. Charles also told him that Jack was a good student with impressive study habits, but lately, he and Clara had not been getting on very well. Clara had complained to her husband that Jack was indifferent to her and that when she reprimanded him, as she had on several occasions, Jack would sometimes act disrespectfully. "I would say, 'If you want to talk to Jack don't talk to him excitably, don't hit him.' At times she told me that she was afraid of Jack and that he was sassy. I never found anything wrong, though. Of course, I understood him."[1]

At this point, McRae wasn't sure if they were dealing with a missing person, a kidnapping, or a murder. While he didn't suspect Jack of having anything to do with the woman's disappearance, he thought that Jack knew something about it and could be protecting someone

---

1   Quotes are taken from the inquest held on April 4, 1914.

else. McRae told Charles that they would take Jack to the police station for questioning and that they would return early the next morning to do a thorough search of the house and the garden. Jack asked to put on a pair of pants that were hanging in his room, but when McRae saw they were still wet at the knees, he refused to let him, and seeing a stain on one of Jack's slippers, asked him to remove those as well.

When Jack arrived at the police substation, Inspector Jackson searched him and pulled out a savings bank book from his pants pocket. Checking their records, the officer noted that it was the same numbered book that Charles Millard reported stolen on March 21. McRae and Jackson were convinced that Jack knew more about the disappearance of his mistress than he was saying. In fact, Jack was saying nothing. He spoke and understood English well, but he appeared frightened as the policemen hurled questions at him from behind the iron grating on the door of the stone cell. He looked like he hadn't slept for several nights; his eyes had dark circles under them.

Jack had reason to be afraid. The city had a social order carved out along strict class and race lines. Vancouver was overwhelmingly white, run mostly by Scots, and marked by pockets of people of colour, mostly in the East End. The city's Chinese population could not vote or hold office and were barred from working in professions such as law and medicine. They could enter Canada only by first paying a hefty Head Tax. Jack would also have been well apprised of the riots that took place in Vancouver just seven years earlier when the Asiatic Exclusion League led as many as 5,000 whites on a rampage through the Chinese community, bashing heads and smashing windows. Chinatown was viewed by outsiders as a place of immorality and sin, where gambling and prostitution thrived and where white women were corrupted by drugs. The Chinese were vilified for their non-Christian beliefs and customs, a supposed lack of hygiene, and a predilection for drugs and criminality. Yet this racist revulsion didn't stop white families from hiring them, mostly because the Chinese worked harder and for less money than their white counterparts. For the Chinese, there was little choice.

McRae decided it was time to put the uncooperative Chinese houseboy through "the third degree," a method of interrogation that was defended in the *Vancouver Sun*, which wrote: "Any method which can be used to extract the truth from the inscrutable Oriental is justifiable." Inspector Jackson read Jack his rights and then questioned him without a lawyer or guardian present. Jack stood with his face turned away from them. Frustrated by Jack's lack of cooperation, McRae yelled at him: "You little whippet. I just feel like throwing you in the inlet. A boy who had been treated as well as you have by Mr and Mrs Millard—to speak to her as you have done, and not to help find those responsible for her disappearance." Jackson told Jack that they were losing time and that he must tell them everything he knew. "You ought to have your block knocked off," Jackson said.[2]

When Jackson returned to the Millard house early the next morning, police officers had already dug up the garden and the yard and searched through the garbage cans. They found several small bones in the furnace ashes. McRae ordered two bloodhounds from the New Westminster penitentiary. When they arrived, the dogs were taken inside and went straight to the breakfast room to sniff at the stained piece of carpet. As the dog handler explained to Jackson, the bloodhound's sense of smell was a thousand times stronger than his. Clara Millard's scent had created a kind of smell photograph in the dogs' brains, and the hounds wouldn't stop until they found her.

Clara's stockings and shoes were brought to the dogs, and they sniffed

---

2 As reported in *The World*, May 19, 1914.

at a chair and then at the base of the chimney. Jackson found a small buckskin bag lodged in the space behind the chimney containing two brooches and a velvet purse with $3.60. A watch and four rings were found wrapped in a piece of school drawing paper which had a maple leaf, figures, and the initials Y.K. (for Yew Kong) printed at the bottom. Charles confirmed that several of the items had been reported stolen in the robbery of March 21.

The dogs took off down the wooden stairs to the basement. The hounds sniffed at an axe, at the furnace, and around the washtubs. After a couple of trips up and down the stairs, the dogs returned to the furnace and sat down.

McRae and Jackson turned their attention to the furnace. It was built so that water could be heated through coils in the firebox. A brick clean-out vent extended to the floor. McRae noticed a sticky material on the side of the furnace. He told Jackson it looked like marrow. Jackson opened the door to the furnace, shook the ashes out of the grate, took everything out, and placed it in a box. After a few minutes, he dug out what looked like pieces of charred bone and bits of steel corset busks, buckles, and garters.

McRae examined the floor in the basement and found cuts in the concrete that looked recent; he thought they'd probably been made by the axe, which, like the floor, looked exceptionally clean. Jackson started to dig around the soot at the base of the chimney; using a long stick, he was able to dislodge a parcel that contained a large portion of a human skull with flesh still attached and what looked like a thigh bone wrapped up in newspaper. By this time, no one doubted that the remains would turn out to be the missing Clara Millard. McRae told an officer to bring Dr Charles McKee, the city's bacteriologist, as well as John F.C.B. Vance, the city analyst, to provide a "chemical analysis of the stuff in the house."

Vance was then a twenty-nine-year-old scientist who worked for the city's health department. His job consisted mostly of analyzing milk for butterfat content, searching for bacteria in food sold commercially, and checking that the city's water supply was safe for human consumption. Vance's knowledge of crime was limited to what he read in newspapers and magazines, occasional visits to the police court in the course of his work, and conversations with police as they came and went from the building.

J.F.C.B Vance. *Courtesy of the Vance family*

Vance arrived with a black suitcase that contained a magnifying glass, flashlight, test tubes, envelopes, and other tools. He took scrapings of the stains and smears from the stairs, the concrete floor in the basement—especially from around the furnace door—and from the baseboards in the breakfast room. He cut out pieces of the baseboard and had these and the other stained items sent to his lab for further analysis.

Back in his lab, Vance laid out two claw-set diamond rings, the axe, a carving knife, a piece from Jack's slipper, the piece of stained carpet, wood from the stairs, a flour bin that had been found on the stairs, and some of the baseboard from the stair landing. Vance knew that even if the carpet had been immediately immersed in water and washed with soap, it would be difficult to eradicate every trace of blood.

The first step was to confirm that the stain was blood, and this required several tests. Vance began by putting each item into cold water.

He would test for haemin crystals, then he would test by tincture of guaiacum, and after that, he would apply the ammonia and the nitric acid tests, which would eliminate any stains that weren't blood. Once the presence of blood was confirmed, Dr McKee would test for human protein to prove without a doubt that the blood was human.

What remained of Clara Millard was transported to the police station and into the care of Dr George Curtis, who attempted to reassemble the incinerated remains into a human frame. Police were no longer looking for a missing person; they were hunting a killer.

Charles Millard asked to be allowed to see Jack, and while that was unusual, McRae decided to let him. Confronted with Clara's stolen bank book, the boy admitted that he was behind the theft on March 21. When the men asked him why he'd done this, he told them that he was angry with the way Mrs Millard had treated him. "During that day, I had a lot of work, and then about night time Mrs Millard was not pleased with the work and she made me angry, and so I went to the room and took these things and hid them away." He had planned to return everything the next day, he said, but when he found out that the Millards had called the police, he believed he'd be sent to jail, so he said nothing.

After hours and hours of relentless questioning, Jack Kong told Charles how his wife had died.

The morning after Charles left for Victoria, Jack got up a little after 6:00 and went down to the basement. He lit the furnace to heat the water then went back to his room in the attic to study. Around 8:00, he went into the kitchen to prepare breakfast for Clara Millard. He laid one place at the breakfast table, then he made toast, oatmeal porridge, and coffee.

The previous day, workers had been at the house replacing the wallpaper in the bedroom, so Clara had slept downstairs. Still dressed in a kimono, she entered the breakfast room and took the seat where her husband normally sat. Jack stopped dusting in the hall to serve her the porridge. They hadn't spoken up to this point, as they only talked to each other when it was unavoidable.

She looked at the porridge. "Oh, Jack, Jack! The very morning Mr Millard is away, you make this porridge, and you know I don't like it," she told him.

Jack told her that he was anxious to get to school on time, and if he made new porridge he'd be late. "I tried to persuade her to take it," Jack later recalled. "She said 'I tell you to take it away. I do not like it. Make the other kind for me.' I said: 'I guess you will have to take it.' She said: 'I do not want you to disobey me.' I said, 'No, my time is limited. I do not see that I have time.' She insisted on me doing it. I thought there wasn't time for me to make the other porridge, and I disobeyed her."

Jack braced himself for his mistress's displeasure. Mr Millard understood his desire to do well in school, but Mrs Millard was "very cranky" about anything that took him away from his domestic chores. Jack thought of her as "very nervous at times," and when she got angry she spoke rapidly and sometimes threw things at him or hit him with a broom.

This particular morning, Clara was furious. She grabbed the carving knife with the white bone handle from the drawer in the buffet and, recalled Jack at his trial, she lunged at him, shouting that she would cut his ear off if he didn't do what she said. She chased him into the kitchen. Jack picked up a chair and pushed it into her shoulder. This only made her angrier, and as she raised the knife Jack hit her with the chair. The edge of the seat caught her on the side of the head and she fell down. Blood flowed from the cut.

"As soon as she fell, I put down the chair to see if I could help her. I put water on her forehead and her mouth. I also tried to stop the bleeding. I called her and she did not answer," Jack said later. "I waited there for a long time to feel if she was breathing again, but no breathing. I know that she must be dead. Then I sat down on the stairs to think."

Jack sat on the landing for about forty-five minutes trying to figure out what to do. He didn't call for help, he said, because he was sure that she was dead, and he was just as sure that Charles Millard would kill him when he returned from Victoria. He decided that since she was already dead, the best chance he had to survive was to get rid of the body and pretend that he didn't know anything about her disappearance.

Clara and Jack were of similar size—about five feet in height and weighing a little over 100 pounds (forty-five kg). Jack put his hands under Clara's arms and hoisted her body onto his back. Placing her arms over his shoulders, he held her with his left hand as he made his way to the stairwell landing. There was no rail on the steep wooden stairs that led down to the basement, so Jack took her in his arms and carried her the rest of the way. Her feet dragged on the steps.

He lay her down on the basement floor, then took off her wedding ring and a smaller opal ring and hid both in a space between the chimney and the wall. Later he said, "I thought she was already dead and I did not want those rings to be burned. I thought I might as well save them and not burn them and spoil any more things."

A fire was still burning in the furnace. Jack added a few pieces of wood to the flames and, taking the axe, chopped off her arms and legs and started to feed body parts into the furnace. He wrapped up the skull and the larger bones that wouldn't burn in a copy of the *Daily Province* and put them in the ashcan until he could dispose of them later. After he had burned most of the body, he put on fresh wood to take away the odour. Then he packed some bloody towels and clothes in a box, walked down the road, and threw them into the water at English Bay.

The gory details of the murder, reported in the local papers, combined

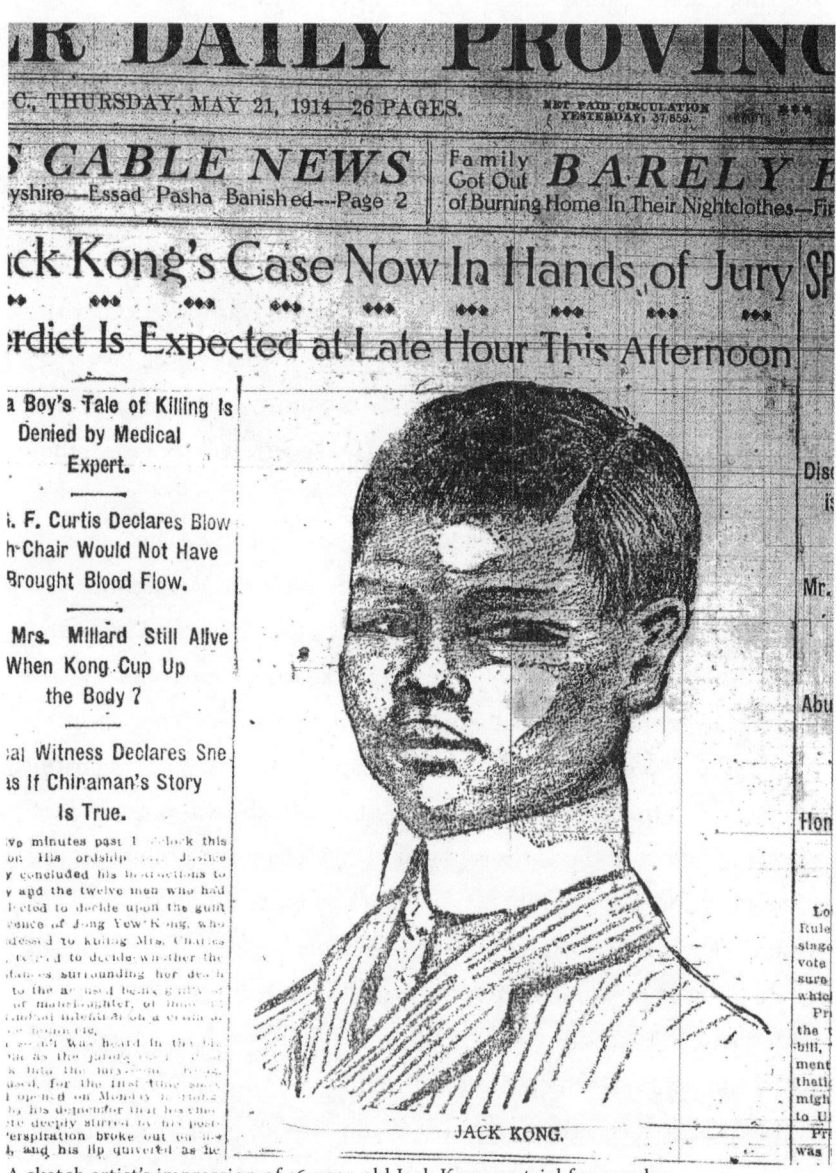

R DAILY PROVIN

C., THURSDAY, MAY 21, 1914—26 PAGES.

NET PAID CIRCULATION
YESTERDAY: 37,859.

S CABLE NEWS | Family Got Out | **BARELY**
yshire—Essad Pasha Banished---Page 2 | of Burning Home In Their Nightclothes—Fi

ck Kong's Case Now In Hands of Jury SP

rdict Is Expected at Late Hour This Afternoon

a Boy's Tale of Killing Is Denied by Medical Expert.

i. F. Curtis Declares Blow h Chair Would Not Have Brought Blood Flow.

Mrs. Millard Still Alive When Kong Cup Up the Body ?

al Witness Declares Sne as If Chinaman's Story Is True.

JACK KONG.

A sketch artist's impression of 16-year-old Jack Kong on trial for murder. *Daily Province*, May 21, 1914.

with news of the impending arrival of the *Komagata Maru* and its 376 mostly Sikh passengers, inflamed anti-Asian panic across the province. For days, headlines such as "Boatload of Hindus on Its Way" fought for space alongside "Chinese Boy Kills White Woman and Burns Body," and "Not Dead When Dissected." These stories titillated and terrified citizens who were now afraid that they'd be overrun by Asians or murdered by their own Chinese houseboys.

The effect on Vancouver's Chinese population was immediate. Chinese men were stopped on the street and beaten. The St. Francis Hotel on Seymour Street publicly fired every Chinese man on staff and dozens of Chinese boys were dismissed from their employment in hotels, restaurants, and private homes. The Trades and Labour Congress tried to have all Asians banned from working in hotels.

One newspaper speculated that Jack was a member of a secret organization of Chinese engaged in teaching anarchism and communism, while others demanded immediate segregation in the schools. "A Chinaman's face as a rule is as expressive as a steam radiator. No one can tell by looking at him what is passing in his mind," reported the *Vancouver Sun*. "This awful tragedy should teach the school board that their first duty is to segregate the Orientals from white children in all the schools."

Council suggested that the city not award contracts to suppliers who employed Asians, clearly having forgotten the general strike by the Chinese after the anti-Asian riots of 1907, which effectively shut down mills and many of the city's restaurants and bars, as well as leaving wealthy householders to fend for themselves.

On May 18, people were lined up outside the courtroom for two hours before the start of Jack's trial. When the doors opened, the crowd consisted of a mix of Shaughnessy Heights matrons, West End women, and Chinese, Japanese, and Indo-Canadians. The crowd crushed and jostled their way up the steps to the court to get seats. As the *World* reported: "Women young and old with the lust of sensationalism in their eyes and lunches in their hands were there prepared to make a picnic of the afternoon." Once all the seats were taken, the doors were closed on the dense crowd that still waited outside, hoping to squeeze past the police guards.

Jack was brought up from the police cells and seated alongside a constable. Dressed in short grey pants, a collar, and tie, he looked even younger than the sixteen-year-old he was. He gazed around the crowded room.

The trial ran for four days and heard from a slew of witnesses including Charles Millard, the Millards' neighbour Margaret Wallace, John F.C.B. Vance, and Jack himself. The lawyer representing Jack was Alex Henderson, a King's Counsel and savvy politician who had served as Attorney General.[3] While the details of the trial were grisly enough, and his admission to the earlier robbery made Jack look bad, the prosecution were leaving nothing to chance. Prosecutor J.K. Kennedy was gunning for the death penalty.

Kennedy argued that Jack had stabbed Clara Millard and was using the chair as a cover-up story. Henderson counter-argued that his client had no motive for murder. Jack, he said, was truly afraid that the woman would cut off his ear or worse, and when Mr Millard found out what happened, Jack feared he would kill him. It was only natural, Henderson said, that Jack would want to cover up the evidence of his crime, in this case, by carrying the body to the basement and burning a large portion of it in the furnace. "That was a fatal inspiration," he told the jury. "For, gentlemen, had he not destroyed those traces, had

---

3 Ten years later, he would be embroiled in the sensational Janet Smith murder that also involved a Chinese houseboy—although this time he would represent the interests of the Scottish community.

he left the body in the breakfast room and called for help, would he now be on trial for murder or for manslaughter?"

Dr George Curtis told the court that he believed that Clara was still alive when she was dismembered. He was basing this, he said, on evidence that Jack had given that there was a "smattering of blood" when he started to cut up the body. Later, under cross-examination, he admitted that a small amount of blood could still seep out of a body after it was dead, but the headlines were already written and it was likely that all the jury would remember was that the woman may have been alive when Jack started to hack her up. Then jurors were shown various exhibits, including the axe, the charred skull, and some bones with flesh still attached. Police had to lock the courtroom doors during lunch time to keep the curious spectators from handling the exhibits and taking souvenirs.

Jack's father Yick Kong added drama to the trial when he chose to take the traditional Chinese Fire Oath in which details of the witnesses' testimony are written on a piece of parchment and then set on fire. As the paper burns, the witness swears to tell the truth on pain of disgracing his ancestors.

When the trial wrapped up, the jury was given three choices: guilty of murder, guilty of manslaughter, or not guilty.

In spite of the graphic and sensational details of the trial, the anti-Asian sentiment of the time, the inflammatory headlines in the media, and the public's desire for a lynching, the jury deliberated for more than seven hours and found Jack guilty of manslaughter. In sentencing Jack, the judge told him that even though the jury found him guilty of manslaughter, he believed Jack should have been convicted of murder and received the death penalty. "After having considered the evidence, I cannot find any extenuating circumstances in the case which should lead me to impose a lesser penalty. On the contrary, I find that your crime was characterized by almost unparalleled cunning and ferocity. The sentence of the court is that you be confined in the penitentiary for the term of your natural life."

By then, however, the sensational murder case had been eclipsed by the assassination of Archduke Franz Ferdinand in Sarajevo, Bosnia, two days earlier. Charles Millard retired from the CPR in 1938 and lived the rest of his life at the Terminal City Club on West Hastings. Yick Kong died in 1919 aged forty-two. Jack, according to Paul Yee's book *Saltwater City*, served only eight years of his life sentence (archival documents do not reveal why his sentence was shortened) and returned to China in 1922. As for J.F.C.B. Vance—the city analyst's career would never be the same again.

THE ANALYST 2

May 1, 1907 was John F.C.B. Vance's first day of work as city analyst. He decided to take the streetcar to City Hall, and as he strode along the raised wooden sidewalks of Smithe Street, he saw that even this early on a Wednesday morning, the city was awake. Vance turned down Granville Street, narrowly missing a man on a bicycle who sped past him, kicking up dust from the dirt road.

A banner stretched across Granville Street boasting that: "In 1910, Vancouver then will have 100,000 men," and apart from the odd syntax, it didn't seem overly optimistic. The city's population had exploded since Vance had arrived as a twelve-year-old just over a decade before, and was now home to 70,000 people.

Still from the first film shot in Vancouver by William Harbeck in 1907 from the front of a streetcar travelling north on Granville Street. *City Reflections team, Vancouver Historical Society*

Vance made it to the Granville and Georgia Street stop just minutes before the tram pulled up. The corner was the social hub of the city, flanked by the sixty-room Hotel Vancouver and the Opera House, both built by the Canadian Pacific Railway. The imposing Hudson's Bay department store had stood across the intersection in a red brick building since 1893.

Vance paid the nickel fare and took a seat just as the conductor called "All aboard" and pulled two clangs on the bell rope. Vance turned

Looking south along Granville Street from Hastings Street, c.1908. *Vancouver Archives 677-585*

to see the motorman spin the brass wheel that released the brakes, and the streetcar was away. There was no glass in the windows, so he felt the cool spring air on his face.

Granville Street was alive with people walking and bicycling, and everyone wore hats. Women glided along in long dark skirts and horses pulled carts and buggies. The CPR terminal—a beautiful chateau-style building that had opened just eight years before—dominated the view at the foot of Granville. The street car took a sweeping turn east along Hastings Street where Vance saw construction on every block. The new post office was going up at Hastings and Granville, and there were large storage sheds on the roads outside the sites. Retail business was booming and banks were putting up substantial multi-storey buildings made of stone and brick.

Vancouver was the financial and transportation centre of the province, outdoing New Westminster and Victoria with its expanding economy, and the city attracted visitors and investors from around the world. Responding to the promise of vast resources, land, and riches, more people arrived every week by boat and train to get a piece of the action. Speculators were already pushing land prices to ridiculous heights, and the CPR was on the verge of opening up huge tracts of land in the new neighbourhood of Shaughnessy to sell to the rich.

The streetcar rattled along Hastings Street, past the Courthouse at Cambie Street and the offices of the *Daily Province*, one of three daily newspapers that collectively employed more than 100 people. The *Province* sold for five cents and bragged that it was read in ninety percent of Vancouver's homes. The *News-Advertiser* hit the streets each morning from its offices on Pender and Hamilton, while the *World* operated out of 426 Homer Street in a building designed by Samuel Maclure and Richard Sharp in 1892.

At Carrall Street, the streetcar stopped to give way to the Interurban train. Vance got ready to disembark outside the Carnegie Library at Westminster Avenue and start his first day at Market Hall, a Gothic turreted building which also doubled as Vancouver City Hall. Vance's lab was in a little room at the top of the tower.

The Vance family had arrived in British Columbia from Alexandria, Scotland, in 1890. Young John turned six on the voyage where he'd been accompanied by his older sister Jean and younger brothers Thomas and James. The Vances' youngest child Frank would be born in Wellington, just north of Nanaimo, on Vancouver Island in 1892.

Like many of his countrymen, John Vance senior had heard all about the great opportunities for those working at Robert Dunsmuir's Vancouver Island coal mines. He lasted for six years as a miner before the dream faded. Vance then moved his family to Vancouver where he took a job with the city. By 1907, when young John started work as the city

Vance's first lab was in Market Hall on Westminster Avenue (now Main Street). The building housed Vancouver City Hall until 1928. *Vancouver Archives 1376-88*

analyst, the Vances were all living in a house at Nelson and Homer Streets. Thomas was a fitter's helper for the CPR, and James worked as a printer.

Young John Vance had worked for various mines since he was seventeen. He'd started as an assistant assayer and soon became an assistant chemist at the War Eagle Cyanide Extraction Plant in Trail, BC, where he developed a cone hood for a hot blast furnace, a breakthrough in metallurgy at the time. Vance became the chief assayer at the Van Anda Mines and Smelter on Texada Island, and worked for a time at the Lucky Boy Mining Company in Blue River, Oregon, before heading to the Kamloops Mines back in BC.

Vance received a certificate in sampling and assaying from the Department of Mines in 1904. It would prove to be essential in his future work as a forensic investigator. It was also fortuitous that the laboratory at the Department of Mines had provided blood identification services since 1890. By the early 1900s, the lab had added toxicology testing to its services, one of the first to do so in North America.

In the spring of 1907, Vance was between mining jobs when Dr Fred Underhill offered him the job of city analyst. Underhill became the City of Vancouver's first medical health officer when he took the job three years earlier, and he was a strong advocate for hygiene and preventative medicine. Underhill had a staff of four—Joseph Hynes, the sanitation inspector, R.H. Meek, milk and food inspector, Joseph Pitman, infectious diseases officer, and his new analyst, Vance. Underhill was impressed with the young man's intelligence and his expertise in chemistry and metallurgy, which he had learned almost entirely on the job.

Dr Underhill gave Vance a tour of the lab as he explained Vance's duties, then returned to his own office, two doors down the corridor. Standing in the centre of the room, Vance let his gaze roam over the little lab. There wasn't much equipment in that room, and it didn't take long to itemize the contents, but it was enough for the work he was required to do.

For the next couple of years, Vance worked from the lab at City Hall without assistance. As the population of Vancouver grew, so did the dairies, flour mills, bakeries, and canneries, all manufacturing goods for human

In 1914 the Vancouver Police Department moved into a new building at 236 East Cordova. Vance's lab was on the top floor. *Vancouver Archives 371-2129*

consumption. Increasingly, Vance was called in by wholesalers to test suspicious food products. From time to time, the Board of Works would ask him to analyze samples of cement, asphalt, and road oils. And twice a week tests had to be made of the water supply at Capilano Canyon and Seymour Creek because Dr Underhill feared a typhoid outbreak. "The great thing in running a health department is never to be satisfied with conditions as they are," he would say.

Underhill was a progressive boss for the times, ensuring that public health care extended to all of Vancouver's citizens. He was vigilant about the cleanliness of food handlers and restaurant kitchens, and he and Vance worked closely together, often taking tours of inspection through the restaurants of Vancouver and the nooks and crannies of Chinatown.

Within a few years, it became clear that the small lab at City Hall was inadequate for the growing services that it provided. More equipment was required and more space to house the equipment. Even more pressing, Vance needed help. Space was found at the Vancouver City Hospital at Cambie and West Pender, and Vance found himself and his new assistant in a lab three times the size of the old one.

Vance was still employed by the Health Department, but he was increasingly doing work for the police. When the Vancouver Police Department moved into a new steel-and-brick building on East Cordova Street, Vance and his lab took over the top floor. The police headquarters was a stunning building, with a huge stained-glass window above a wide marble staircase that led to second-floor courtrooms, chambers, and witness rooms. Prisoners were transported from the large jail upstairs to the courtrooms by a separate interior staircase. The building also had elevators, a gym, a tailor shop, and a kitchen in which prisoners' meals were prepared.

On April 3, 1914, when Vance entered the Millards' West End home and took samples of stains to determine their origin, forensic science in police work was still in its infancy. In those early days, forensics mostly involved toxicology because poison was a frequent cause of death either by choice, accident, or murder. The first government-funded forensic science lab for North America had opened in Montreal earlier that year, and it conducted autopsies, biological tests, and fingerprint and firearms examinations. Professor Henry Holmes Croft of Toronto was the first forensic chemist in Canada. He had made history in 1859 when he testified at the trial of Dr William Henry King for the murder of his wife Sarah. Professor Croft tested her stomach, liver, and kidneys for arsenic and testified that he'd found eleven grains in her stomach—not enough to cause her death. The jury convicted King of murder anyway, and the doctor was sentenced to death. It turned out that Professor Croft was correct; Dr King had not murdered his wife with arsenic. As he was led up to the gallows, he confessed to murdering his wife with morphine.

The next forensic breakthrough in Canada came during a rape and murder case in 1878. William Hodgson Ellis, a medical doctor and chemist, identified the presence of human blood and testified to the significance of the number, size, and position of blood stains on the pants of the accused man (early blood spatter analysis). By 1914, scientists could identify a stain, prove that it was blood, determine if it was human, and identify its ABO blood group.

While work and home life were increasingly busy for Vance, in 1914 the Great War began to occupy his thoughts. He joined the Vancouver Volunteer Reserve as a platoon sergeant, and for the next two years waged his own war trying to get permission to serve at the front. At one point, he even attempted to resign from his job to do so. When that was stymied in 1916 by Police Chief Malcolm McLennan, Mayor L.D. Taylor and his successor, Malcolm McBeath, Vance wrote to the Minister of Militia in Ottawa:

Ever since the outbreak of War in 1914 I have tried to enlist in different local regiments, but on each occasion, have been asked to wait. I am anxious to proceed overseas in any capacity. I have been giving my spare time since the end of 1914 in experimental work in connection with gases in use in the war under the Chemical Society of England, in analyses of machine gun sections under the Canadian Government, have examined and inspected all foods passing through Vancouver for the overseas forces and all the analyses and examinations for the local Corps including the army service, the military intelligence, the regiments while stationed here, and I have done this without any charge whatever.

In the end, Vance never left his lab. Instead he was given a fifty-dollar-a-month raise largely to compensate for the extra work he had to do after losing his assistant to the war. He worked at least six days a week, often late into the night, and it wasn't unusual to see him in his lab on a Sunday. By the end of 1917, half of his time was spent on work for the health department; police work took up another forty percent, and the balance was spent on work for the Board of Works and the Water Department.

Visitors to the lab were met with an array of exhibits and equipment. There were long rows of retorts and glass test tubes, instruments with polished brass dials, scales that gave the exact weight of a tiny speck of dirt, and various other contrivances to analyze everything from the milk Vancouverites drank to the quality of the asphalt that went into paving the streets. City water still had to be tested weekly, and samples were taken daily. On any day, Vance and his assistants could be testing a pinch of powder to determine whether it was aspirin or cocaine, examining a human stomach for traces of poison, inspecting blood stains in a murder case, or analyzing the nitroglycerin used by "yeggs" (safecrackers) in a robbery.

Vance's expertise in firearms examination grew, and he spent a lot of his time in the courtroom. Back in the office, Vance's library was expanding. Among his chemistry books and sanitary health journals were works by forensic scientists from around the world, with titles such as *Modern Criminal Investigation*, *The Laboratory Detective*, *Murder in All Ages*, *The Underworld Speaks*, and *The Scientific Detective and the Expert Witness*.

Part of the city analyst's duties included working with breweries to ensure that the water they used was not polluted, as well as testing hundreds of samples of alcoholic beverages suspected of being above or below the legal standards. When the BC government legislated Prohibition in October 1917, alcohol testing took on a prominent role. Bootlegging had evolved from a cottage industry to a business opportunity for organized crime. "Blind pigs"—rundown illegal drinking and gambling dens—sprang up all over the city.

Prohibition proved to be a cash cow for the government as fines received by the city treasury from those caught making or selling illegal booze reached $12,000 a month. One of the many loopholes in the act was the allowance for "near-beer" bars that could sell liquor with a maximum concentration of two-and-a-half percent alcohol by volume. Before the government could collect their fines, samples of the products had to be analyzed by Vance and his assistant and proven to be above the legal limit.

Joe Ricci and his partner Donald Sinclair were two of the busiest detectives on the force. They had a talent for capturing illicit stills hidden away in attics and cellars and in bars and outhouses in the woods surrounding Vancouver. The stills ranged from small producers to those that could turn out fifty gallons a day of whiskey made from everything from parsnips and turnips to grape seeds. After these raids, Vance's lab would be flooded with moonshine to test.

Det. Joe Ricci, James Thorburn, deputy-collector, Inland Revenue Department, and Det. Donald Sinclair with captured liquor stills, c.1917. *Vancouver Archives 480-215*

Ricci, the Vancouver Police Department's first Italian detective, was a familiar sight on city streets in his pinstripe suit and Borsalino hat. The detective would hand Vance the confiscated booze, and he would issue a receipt. He would then divide each sample into three parts, returning a part to the detective. The second part he put aside for future reference in the case of a dispute. Vance would distill the alcohol from the third part and weigh it. He compared the weight of pure alcohol with that of the liquid form and made out a certificate, which he would produce when called to testify in court.

More serious than illegal booze was the drug trade, which was then growing in size and organization. By 1919, the city's police department was focussed on eradicating both booze and drugs from Vancouver, and Vance was frequently called in to help with the fight. Often the confiscated "drugs" turned out to be nothing more than baking powder or ground aspirin, but a little glass container in Vance's lab could contain hundreds of dollars worth of cocaine, morphine, or crude opium. Legal in Vancouver until 1908[4] and the drug of choice in Chinatown, opium was typically made into pills or sold in little dark-brown slabs of cheap peanut brittle. Vance also found drugs in fruit and chocolate bars bound for the dance halls.

In the year 1920, Vance's lab made 5,579 examinations of drugs, alcohol, and other materials from suspected murder cases, explosives used by safecrackers, as well as food and liquids. Of these examinations, 3,299 of his reports were introduced as material evidence in police court prosecutions.

Somehow, between 1907 and 1920 the busy analyst also found time to further his qualifications. Vance's credentials included professional engineer in chemical and metallurgical engineering with the Association of Professional Engineers of BC. He was a member of the Pharmaceutical Association of BC, and he was elected a Fellow of the Canadian Institute of Chemistry (FCIC) and a Fellow of the prestigious Chemical Society of England (FCS).

On March 25, 1920, Henry Reifel, the owner of Vancouver Breweries Limited, offered Vance the position of analyst. He would be paid $5,000 a year, more than double his salary with the city. Vance immediately turned down the job, but did use the offer as leverage to ask for a raise of $100 a month from the police department, which would bring his annual salary to $3,600.

---

4 Drug use was criminalized in Canada in 1908 following the passage of the Opium Act, which was indirectly the result of the 1907 Vancouver anti-Asiatic riot. In response to the riot, future prime minister William Lyon Mackenzie King, then deputy minister of labour, arrived in Vancouver to investigate. He was alarmed to find that the Chinese practice of smoking opium was spreading to the white population. The Opium Act prohibited "the importation, manufacture and sale of opium for other than medicinal purposes." In 1911 the charge of smoking opium was added to the revised Opium and Narcotic Drugs Act (ONDA).

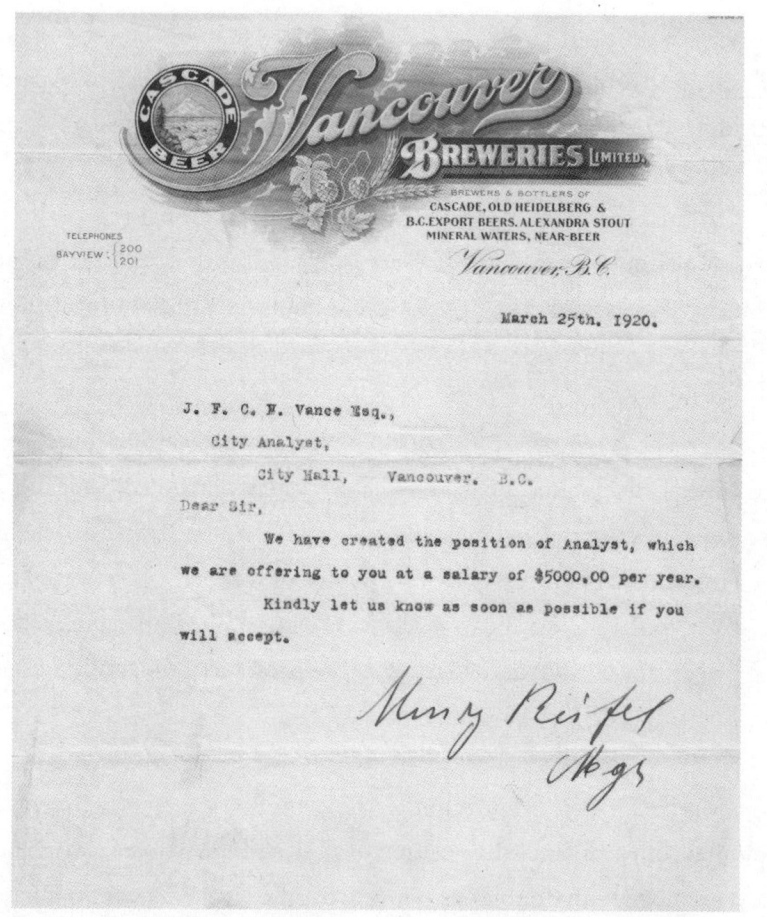

The job offer from Henry Reifel from Vancouver Breweries in 1920 was more than double Vance's salary with the city of Vancouver. *Courtesy of the Vance family*

Five years later, BC Premier John Oliver appointed Vance provincial analyst and analyst for the Liquor Control Board. This additional work meant Vance would notch up a lot of miles travelling around BC and the Yukon.

By the end of 1925, Vance was exhausted and in need of a break. He asked for a one-month leave of absence so that he and his family could investigate health inspection methods in various US cities—not most people's idea of a holiday. An announcement in Vance's local community

THE DAILY PROVINCE, VANCOUVER, BRITIS

Everything from Moonshine to Milk
Must Pass Searching Test of City Analyst

J. F. C. Vance's Skill May Save Man From Gallows.

Few Tricks of Narcotic Pedlars Hoodwink Him.

By C. O. SCOTT.

CITY ANALYST RUNS CITY'S STILL

"BUSINESS is good," said Mr. J. C. Vance, city analyst, as he put into operation the city's own private still, in his office on the top floor of the police station.

He had a quite a day's work ahead of him. The city detective department had just accepted his receipt for twenty-two beer bottles with something in them. As these samples were secured from bootleggers, Mr. Vance had to make sure the contents were what the labels said they were.

So he divided each sample into three parts, giving the police back one part. The second he put aside for future reference in case of dispute. And the third he placed in his little still, where the water in it soon dissolved in steam and only the alcohol remained. He compared the weight of pure alcohol with that of the liquid from which it came, and made out a certificate for use in court.

Later Mr. Vance must stand in the witness box, identify his bottles, identify his certificates, and answer whatever questions the defense lawyer can use to confound him. Sometimes he has to follow appeal cases to final decision in three courts. For this reason he is absolutely accurate, and must even carry caution to the extent of sealing both label and bottle cap of every exhibit that leaves his office.

Vance's work first came to the attention of the media in the early 1920s. *Daily Province,* March 22, 1924. *Courtesy of the Vance family*

paper, the *North Vancouver Review*, stated: "It is the first holiday Mr Vance has taken in fourteen years, having preferred to remain at work." When he returned to work, it was straight back to six days a week, balancing his duties between forensic investigation, court appearances, and assisting police with cases in Vancouver and throughout the province.

John and Ethel Vance's wedding.
Courtesy of the Vance family

In August 1911, Vance married Ethel Burnes at the Church of St. John the Evangelist in North Vancouver. Vance met his bride, a secretary, at city hall where they both worked. Their first son, John—another in a long line of John Vances but known as Jack throughout his life—was born in 1912. Tom followed in 1913, Marian in 1918, and Caroline (called by her middle name Edith) in 1926. The boys went to North Vancouver High, while the girls attended the Crofton House School for girls in the West End. The Vances raised their family in North Vancouver at 862 Cumberland Street. The Craftsman-style house is listed in Canada's Historic Places, and while the social history doesn't mention the Vance family, it does say that in the 1930s,

862 Cumberland Street. *Eve Lazarus photo, 2017*

Thomas Hooper, the architect who once had practices in three cities and designed Hycroft Manor in Shaughnessy and the Royal Bank in Victoria, spent his retirement years in this house.

JAPATOWN

By 1931, the Great Depression was two years old and had firmly taken hold of Vancouver. Workers lost their jobs or had their paycheques slashed. Thousands of unemployed Canadians flocked to the warmer climate of Vancouver in search of work—only to further deplete an already inadequate relief system. The size of the city's homeless population grew, and hobo jungles sprang up around the False Creek Flats, near the city dump between Campbell and Heatley in Strathcona, underneath the original Georgia Viaduct, and at the old Hastings Mill site at the foot of Dunlevy Street.

While conditions were bad all over, they were worse for the Japanese, who were paid only a fraction of the social assistance paid to whites. The sick and indigent had even fewer options.

Shinkichi Sakurada, a forty-year-old sawmill worker, had a house on East Cordova Street in "Japantown," an enclave that stretched almost from the doorstep of Vance's downtown lab to the waterfront and up along Jackson Street past the Powell Street Grounds (now Oppenheimer Park). The area was close to the Hastings Sawmill, which employed predominately Japanese workers. There were Japanese shops, hotels, restaurants, a Buddhist church, a language school, and dozens of rooming houses that offered shelter to the destitute for a couple of quarters a night.

Sakurada had turned his house into a private hospital and was known in the community as a "medicine man" even though he had no medical training. Perhaps because his hospital's sign was in Japanese and the illegal services he provided there were known only to the Japanese

Two Japanese-Canadian children outside the Bunka Shokai store on Powell Street in 1928. *Vancouver Public Library #21773*

community, it went undetected by police and the rules and bylaws of the City Health Department, which employed Vance.

It was a little after 11:00 p.m. on March 29, 1931, when Bunshiro Fujino, a thirty-seven-year-old insurance agent, returned to his house on Powell Street after visiting a friend. He'd just managed to take off his coat when there was a knock on the door. His friend Sakurada came in wearing a raincoat, carrying an umbrella, and dripping water on the floor. Sakurada asked Fujino if he had seen Naokichi Watanabe, who was in poor health and being taken care of at his hospital. Fujino told him he had not seen Watanabe that night.

Sakurada told Fujino that he'd loaned Watanabe thirty dollars earlier that evening, and when he had not returned three hours later, he'd become worried. Sakurada went out to look for Watanabe at the Japanese bath-house and then phoned a few of his friends. No one had seen Watanabe. He told Fujino that he suspected Watanabe had gone to see his friend "Jimmy" Yamashita, a fisherman who lived on his gillnetter moored at the old Hastings Mill wharf, and asked him to accompany him there. Fujino reluctantly put on his damp raincoat and followed Sakurada down Cordova Street and then north along Heatley Avenue to the waterfront. When they found Yamashita, he told them that he had not seen Watanabe that night.

It was now after 1:00 in the morning, and Fujino was angry with Sakurada and just wanted to go home. The two men walked back along the railway tracks past a long line of freight cars. Fujino was walking along a steep bank when Sakurada called out to him and pointed to a dark object lying on the CPR tracks at the back of the American Can Company's plant on Railway Street. Sakurada lit a match and saw that it was a corpse lying face-up with legs outstretched. He took off his scarf and placed it over the badly beaten head and then covered the body with his raincoat.

"It's Watanabe," he told Fujino. "Get the police. I'll wait here."

"You have put me in a bad position this time," Fujino told Sakurada. And Sakurada answered, "I quite appreciate what I have done." Sakurada promised Fujino that he would receive a cut from Watanabe's insurance money for his trouble.

Fujino returned with detectives Charles Spence and Harry Duggan who had the forethought to bring a large flashlight. It was still raining heavily and pitch-dark. "I got out of the car and started to look around, and I could not see more than ten or twelve feet in front of me," said Duggan at the inquest. "Suddenly, I saw what appeared to be a man

A funeral procession in front of Japanese Methodist Mission at Jackson and Powell Streets in the late 1920s. *Vancouver Archives PAN N143A*

rising up from the ground, holding an umbrella. I walked across to where I saw this man, and I saw the body of Watanabe."

When Duggan lifted up the scarf, he saw that the man's throat was cut, and he could see that part of the bone in his chin was missing from another slash. Another blow had almost severed his ear, and he had a stab wound in the middle of his forehead. The right side of his head was bashed in where it had been pounded by something heavy like an axe. Duggan searched the body and found all the pockets empty except for $3.85 stuffed in the small pocket at the waist of his pants.

Forty-nine-year-old Naokichi Watanabe had left Japan for Vancouver two decades before. He'd suffered a back injury the previous year that had left him partially disabled. Sakurada had loaned Watanabe some money because, as he told people, Watanabe was hard up and had no friends or relatives in Vancouver. Sakurada then helped Watanabe take out an insurance policy on his life for $2,500, naming himself as Watanabe's beneficiary.

Watanabe was owed $1,000 from the Workmen's Compensation Board and earlier that month had received a partial payment of $293. He gave Harry Keno (a.k.a. Fred Yoshi) ninety dollars to purchase a ticket so that Watanabe could return to Japan. The agreement with the

Compensation Board said that Watanabe would receive the balance of $700 on confirmation of his arrival in Japan.

When the detectives found out that Sakurada was the beneficiary of a life insurance policy that Watanabe had taken out four months earlier and that Fujino was the insurance agent who'd sold it to him, they became suspicious. They raided Sakurada's hospital the morning following the murder and found a stethoscope, a blood pressure "detector," several hypodermic syringes, absorbent cotton, and several bottles that—Vance later confirmed—contained cocaine and morphine. They also found Sam Tsunda lying in a cot, and took the ailing man to St. Paul's Hospital. Tsunda told them that he had gone to Sakurada a month before to be treated for his cough but that his condition had grown worse after Sakurada gave him injections.

The same morning, Tadao Hitomi had come into the police station and reported that he had been attacked and robbed by two men at the corner of Georgia and Beatty Streets. Detective Spence noted that he was extremely agitated and had scratches on his face and a bad gash over his left eye. Later that day, Hitomi turned up at Sakurada's while police were searching his house and got into a conversation with the Japanese interpreter who was working with police. Duggan took Hitomi

Naokichi Watanabe's body was found lying on the CPR tracks behind the American Can Company at the foot of Princess Street. This 1926 photo also shows the Hastings Saw Mill at the bottom of Dunlevy. *Vancouver Public Library #4269*

back to the station. As he was questioning Hitomi, Duggan noticed something sticking out from under his cap. He found a note with Japanese characters, which when translated read: "White police suspect me of murdering Watanabe. I have disgraced the Japanese community. I will die. I will kill myself." When Duggan searched Hitomi, he found a linen sheet tied around his waist, and thought that the man intended to hang himself.

Hitomi was a lean, wiry little man who was considered intellectually disabled. He knew Watanabe and had fished for salmon with him. People who lived in his building told police that they had smelled something odd coming from his room. A Mr Ishii, who lived in the room next door, said that he had loaned Hitomi his hatchet. Police seized two stoves at Hitomi's Powell Street residence, one used for burning oil and the other for coal. The stoves, the ashes, and his clothes were sent to Inspector Vance for examination.

Hitomi quickly broke down under questioning and told police that he had owed both Watanabe and Sakurada money. Sakurada had promised him some of the insurance money as payment for killing Watanabe. Hitomi said that he, Watanabe, and Sakurada had walked down the CPR tracks below Heatley Street. Sakurada engaged

Shinkichi Sakurada's "private hospital" labelled by press as "the murder factory," on East Cordova Street. *Eve Lazarus photo, 2016*

Watanabe in conversation while Hitomi brought out a hatchet that he'd hidden in his coat pocket. He hit Watanabe on the neck. Watanabe fought back, but Sakurada grabbed his arms. "I struck some more, and he fell down. Sakurada then told me to cut his throat. I shut my eyes and I strike down—ugh! I do not hit his throat, but chop through his chin. I strike again with my eyes shut—ugh! And it is done," he told police. Hitomi then showed police where he had hidden the hatchet and some bloody clothing that he was unable to burn in a large tin can which he'd tossed into a False Creek Flats mud hole at the foot of Heatley Street.

Sakurada and Hitomi were charged with murder. The Crown argued that the two men had murdered Watanabe for the insurance money and done it hastily in their rush to kill Watanabe before he had a chance to return to Japan.

Hitomi and Sakurada were tried separately for the murder. Sakurada testified that he knew nothing of the murder but had arrived to find Hitomi standing over the body of Watanabe. He was afraid to say anything, he said, because Hitomi had threatened his life if he talked. Hitomi's lawyer offered no defence, simply stating that the confession obtained by police was secured under duress and couldn't be admitted as evidence. After Hitomi's testimony, the judge recommended that he be examined because he did not "seem to be in a fit mental condition."

Most damning was the evidence from Fred Yoshi (a.k.a. Harry Keno),[5] the same man whom Watanabe had paid to arrange his passage back to Japan. He told the court that Sakurada had asked him to murder Watanabe and two others whose lives had been insured. Instead of carrying out the crimes, Yoshi said, he had taken the money and fled to Chilliwack, where he was later arrested.

Both Sakurada and Hitomi were found guilty of murder and were hanged on December 30, 1931 at Oakalla Prison Farm.

While the Japanese language newspapers printed detailed accounts of the Watanabe killing or *koroshi*, the mainstream media took little interest until police called Sakurada's modest six-room house, "a murder factory." Insurance company representatives told police that several Japanese citizens who had died, supposedly from natural causes, during the previous two or three years, had been insured through Fujino, and in a few cases, had named Sakurada as the beneficiary. In a story headlined "Murder Syndicate Collects Insurance on Victims'

---

5   Fred Yoshi (also known as Harry Keno, Fred Yoshy, Saburo Yoshiye, and Kiyoshi Sugimoto) was arrested for breach of trust in July 1931. While employed as an interpreter for the Immigration Department, he was suspected of smuggling more than 2,000 Japanese into BC. An investigation found that Yoshi was charging his human cargo as much as $1,000 for a fake birth or naturalization certificate to enable entry into Canada. Yoshi was convicted of conspiracy and unlawfully receiving a gift while employed by the government, fined $100, and sentenced to two years and seven months of hard labour.

Vance with Chief Constable Bingham, c.1930. *Courtesy of the Vance family*

Lives," the *Globe and Mail* reported that police suspected an "organized assassination ring" operated in Japantown and was responsible for as many as twenty deaths.

Other Japanese people came forward with reports of suspicious circumstances surrounding the deaths of friends and relatives. A fisherman named Tomizo Sato said two of his children had died in Sakurada's hospital six months before Watanabe's murder; his daughter Shizue had died from "tuberculosis," and her brother Masamichi had died from "intestinal trouble." Police Chief William Bingham told reporters that he would petition the Attorney General to exhume the bodies, as it was now believed that they may have been poisoned. A few days later, a short article in a local paper mentioned that Bingham had decided not to go through with the exhumation. Judging by the lack of follow-up, the investigation into the murder syndicate died along with Sakurada and Hitomi.

As city analyst, it would have been Vance's job to examine the organs

The Vances bought this Kerrisdale house in 1931 and stayed there until John Vance's retirement in 1949. *Eve Lazarus photo, 2017*

of the victims for poison, but there is no mention of these tests in the VPD report for 1931 or in Vance's own files. It appears that Vance's role was limited to testing the drugs confiscated from the hospital and determining that the stains found on the clothing of Hitomi and on items in his room were human blood.

Vance had been mentioned in newspaper articles, but it was mostly in connection to his work as city analyst —for meat inspections, alcohol testing, and the odd poisoning case, either accidental or intentional. Then, in the spring of 1931, the *Vancouver Sun* ran a story called "Builders of Vancouver," featuring Vance as one of fifty top business leaders in the city. The press was intrigued and began to report on his work in criminology and on his successes in the courtroom.

CANADA'S SHERLOCK HOLMES

While Vance's official job title was still city analyst, and he was still responsible for keeping Vancouver's food, milk, and water safe, those duties were now largely supervisory; the majority of his work came from criminal investigations. A shy man by nature, Vance looked more like a high school history teacher than a policeman, but he was now a familiar figure at crime scenes, and his court appearances were reported by the local media in bold front-page headlines. His success in helping to convict criminals based on scientific evidence garnered attention from outside his hometown, and newspapers as far away as England had taken to calling him "the Sherlock Holmes of Canada." The *Canadian Police Gazette* wrote about Vance's achievements under the headline "Super Criminologist," while *Maclean's* magazine featured him in an article called "Test Tube Detective."

Vancouver was one of the few police departments in North America to have a forensics scientist on staff or progressive enough to take advantage of science in its investigations, and certainly in Canada there was little else available. The original forensic science lab that

In 1934 Vance was persuaded to loan his museum of crime-solving apparatus and exhibits to the Canada Pacific Exhibition, and later that year, to BC Electric Railway's showroom. *Courtesy of the Vance family*

opened in Montreal in 1914 was still operating, and a much smaller lab had opened in Toronto in 1932. Western Canada wouldn't get a police science lab for another five years, when the RCMP opened the Crime Detection Lab in an attic bedroom in an officers' mess in Regina in 1937. The RCMP didn't open a lab in Vancouver until 1963. Vance and his lab were on the cutting edge of forensic science in North America, and in the 1930s, he began to receive requests for assistance from police departments and the RCMP from all over the province.

In June 1932, the Dawson City RCMP asked Vance to assist in the identification and classification of blood stains on some clothing found in connection with the murder of Michael Essanasa, a retired miner known to keep large sums of money in his cabin because he didn't trust the banks. He'd been found in his cabin beaten to death. Barney West, a forty-seven-year-old meat cutter who worked in a butcher store in Dawson, came under suspicion after suddenly paying off all his overdue bills and buying jewellery for his girlfriend.

The problem for the RCMP was that West said that the blood stains on his clothes were from animals that he'd cut up in the course of his work. Vance was able to prove that not only was the blood on his clothes human, it was from the same blood group as Essanasa's. When confronted with this evidence in court, West changed his plea to guilty and confessed to beating Essanasa over the head with a piece of lead pipe and a bag filled with shot and stealing $850 from him. West received the death penalty, and on September 27, 1932, had the distinction of being the last person hanged in the Yukon.

Vance finally got the recognition he deserved in November 1932 when Police Chief Charles Edgett gave him the title of honorary inspector and put him in charge of the newly formed Police Bureau of Science. The same year, the FBI officially opened its crime laboratory in Washington, DC. Vance's new 6,000-square-foot (557-square-meter)

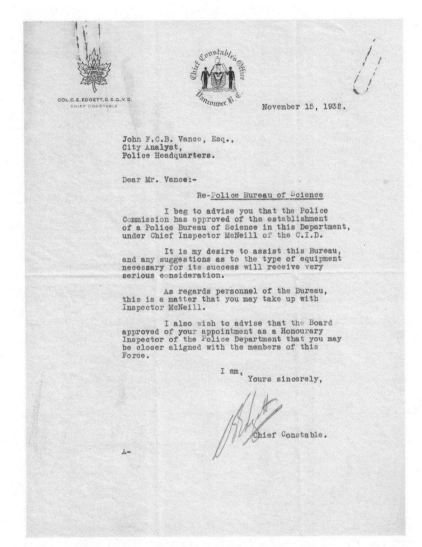

Vance is appointed honorary inspector of the newly created Police Bureau of Science in November 1932. *Courtesy of the Vance family*

lab was built to his specifications and was one of the largest and best equipped police sciences labs in North America. He was assisted by Detective Horace Vince, a veteran police officer with experience in the police's identification bureau. A story in the *Daily Province* of June

COL.C.E.EDGETT. D.S.O.V.D.
CHIEF CONSTABLE

November 25, 1932.

GENERAL ORDER #127.

    A new field of scientific crime detection has been opened up with the establishment of the VANCOUVER POLICE BUREAU OF SCIENCE, under the administration and control of Mr. J.F.C.B. Vance, City Analyst.

    In order to have an opportunity of formulating instructions regarding preservation of evidence, and of observing the type of evidential matter available in such cases, Mr. Vance would like to be called upon when cases occur wherever his services are likely to be of assistance to those investigating. He can be notified by day at his office, or after office hours, at his home at 6626 Adera Street, Kerrisdale 3190L.

    Pending publication of such instructions, the following should be borne in mind:

    Weapons; Burglars' Tools, or other articles associated with the commission of a crime should be kept UNTOUCHED until arrival of Mr. Vance, or Detective Vince. Officers should meantime guard the immediate environs from intrusion by curious spectators, because their presence may result in the destruction of microscopic matter of value to the Science Bureau, but hitherto overlooked as unimportant.

    This course should be particularly adhered to in the cases of bodies found under circumstances which suggest the possibility of foul-play. If it is established that the victim is beyond human aid, the body should be left as discovered, and nothing in the immediate vicinity should be handled or disturbed until Mr. Vance has attended and conducted his examination.

    Automobiles used in hold-ups, etc., and afterwards abandoned, should also be guarded and preserved in the condition in which found. They should not be entered or searched nor should the steering-gear be handled prior to examination by members of science Bureau; unless unavoidable in the interests of public safety.

               By Order
               (signed) C. E. Edgett
                      Chief Constable.

Chief Constable Edgett instructs police as to the requirements of the newly created Police Bureau of Science. *Courtesy of the Vance family*

1933 called Vance's department "the only bureau of its kind in Canada and the only one of its size outside of England or France."

The building was repurposed in 1986 as the Vancouver Police Museum, but five decades earlier, Vance had already co-opted a section of the lab for exhibits. In 1932, the first thing a visitor to Vance's lab would notice were shelves displaying a strange collection of "live bombs," narcotics, counterfeiting equipment, safecrackers' tools, blood-stained clothes, a noose, a gown worn by an executioner, and the uniform of Malcolm McLennan, the chief of police who was shot and killed by a drug addict in 1917.

In 1934, Vance was persuaded to loan his exhibits to the Canada Pacific Exhibition, the forerunner to the Pacific National Exhibition (PNE), and later that year his crime-solving apparatus went on display at BC Electric Railway's showroom. The exhibit—carefully guarded and insured for $10,000—included large photographs that showed Vance at work with his microscopes and test tubes.

Vance's lab was packed with all the latest gear in forensics. In the early days he worked with a polarimeter for identifying liquids; a spectroscope for examining blood, smears, and stains; a refractometer for examining liquids and drugs; and a fine scale for weighing poisons obtained from victims' bodies. To his new lab, Vance added a comparator for analyzing handwriting, typewriting, and fingerprints; a comparison microscope to identify firearms; and another microscope for identifying minute particles of dust, hair, wood splinters, and fabric left behind at crime scenes. When Vance couldn't buy the equipment he needed, he'd either adapt the tools he had or invent something new.

In 1931, the *Daily Province* reported on a new addition to the lab—a piece of "crime-fighting" equipment that the media immediately dubbed "the Robot Detective." Ultra-violet rays, also known as black light, were used to detect everything from forged documents to drugs and bodily fluids. Vance had designed a portable ultra-violet ray lamp that could be used by police at crime scenes. Blood stains, saliva, semen, vaginal fluids, urine, and perspiration all fluoresce under ultra-violet light, which made it easier to pick out footprints and fingerprints at

Vance's experiments with forensic odours cemented his reputation as Canada's Sherlock Holmes. *Vancouver Province*, July 7, 1934. *Courtesy of the Vance family*

a crime scene. "We can also use this for suspected counterfeit money or forged cheques because different inks glow with different colours in the rays," Vance told a reporter. "Any additions or changes in the cheque will be immediately noted under the ray by their failure to glow with the same colour."

But the machine he began to design in 1927, and the one that the media was calling "the robot nose," was his obsession.

Vance had a theory that everyone had an individual odour which, like a fingerprint, was distinctive, perhaps unique. He described his invention as a "mechanical bloodhound," because he believed it would act the same way as a bloodhound does in tracking its quarry. The machine he developed essentially gave smell a physical form; it could detect, capture, and record individual human smells. The "mechanical bloodhound" was small, about the size of a news photographer's camera. It looked like an elongated shadow box with a glass cover and two handles at the upper end. The lower end was open. By 1932,

Vance had started trials, and if they proved successful, it could make investigators' reliance on fingerprints obsolete, just as fingerprints had improved upon and then surpassed the Bertillon measurement system.[6]

Vance had discovered that skin pigmentation varied greatly from person to person. Criminals, he surmised, could be identified by pigmentation cells from the surface of the skin that were left at the crime scene. The pigmentation carried distinctive odours that remained for some time after a hand or foot touched a surface. Most interesting to Vance was that his invention could detect individual odours on a surface even when they came from a person wearing shoes or gloves. In December 1934, the *Canadian Police Gazette* wrote about Vance's invention and described the process as follows: "Chemicals sprayed over the spot where a suspect is believed to have stood rise into the lower end of the instrument and strike a spectrum band. Pointers indicate where the band has been broken. It is claimed that no two persons have the same spectrum record, hence classification is as sure as that of fingerprints."

After eight decades of scientific advances, it's easy to look back at Vance's theory with incredulity, but in 1934 identification by odour seemed not only possible but exciting, and the story of Vance's "mechanical bloodhound" quickly gained traction outside of Vancouver. Vance and Vancouver's Police Bureau of Science received worldwide attention from the media as well as from scientists and police departments. Vance's reputation as the "Sherlock Holmes of Canada" grew.

Douglas M. Lucas, former director of the Centre of Forensic Sciences in Ontario, says he knows of many attempts over the years in

---

6 Alphonse Bertillon, a French criminologist, developed the first organized system for identifying individuals in 1879 after he discovered that every individual had a unique combination of measurements of different body parts. It was labour intensive, not always accurate, and was eventually replaced by fingerprinting in the early 20th century.

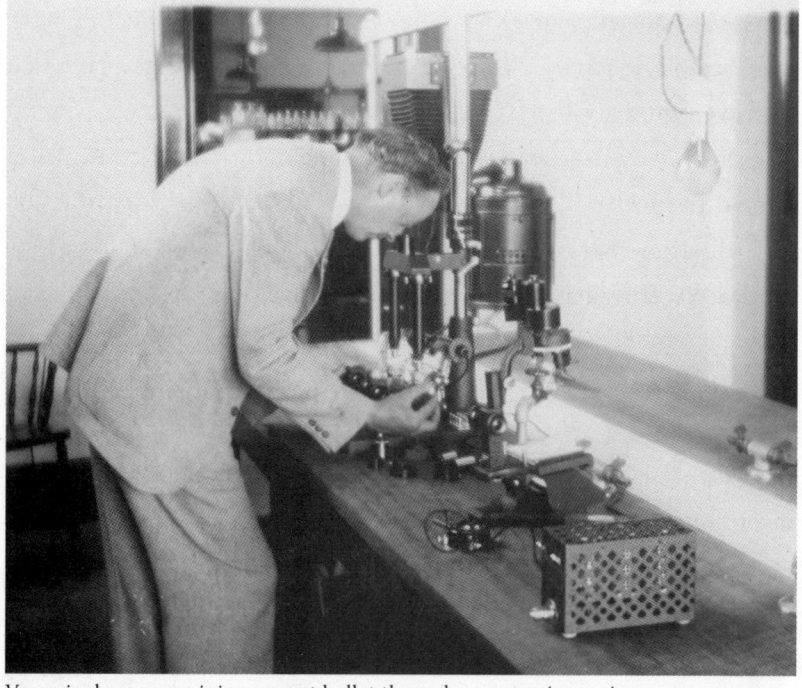

Vance is shown examining a spent bullet through a comparison microscope, c.1932. The comparison microscope included a camera for photographing images of the matching bullets or cartridge cases. *Courtesy of the Vance family*

which researchers have tried to detect different odours with far more sophisticated equipment than Vance would have access to when he started experimenting in 1927 or even when he retired in 1949. "Yes, people do have different odours, but they don't stay the same," says Lucas. "The odour that you have today—depending on what you had for dinner last night—might be different than what you will have next week, so you couldn't use it for identification purposes because it's just not a permanent sort of thing."

Fingerprints, on the other hand, have stayed the course for identification purposes because they do not change as a person ages. DNA, which didn't arrive in the forensic tool bag until the 1980s, is also highly effective, because the criminal leaves something physical behind.

"An odour is a much more transitory type of thing," says Lucas.

"It would disappear quickly, and it could be interfered with just as quickly. The problem is, if your technique is sensitive enough to pick up the scent of someone, whose scent is it going to be? It could be from the first police officer who walked into the room after the body was discovered."

When he wasn't working on his inventions, Vance spent much of his time reconstructing crime scenes in the lab. He knew there was no room for scientific error when he presented his findings in court, but he also needed to be able to walk the judge and the jury through the events that took place so they could almost see it.

Often police had a suspect but only circumstantial evidence. Tiny pieces of glass, grains of dust or soil, and strands of hair or fibre could be the evidence that would either confirm a suspect's presence at the scene or exonerate him from the crime. Vance could make bits of clay or gravel or blood-stained clothes talk to him and to the jury. When detectives found a burned-out shell of a car that they suspected had hit and killed two people, Vance was able to prove they had the right car by demonstrating how the particles of glass found on the road near the bodies fit perfectly into a tiny, hardly noticeable hole in one of the headlights of the damaged car.

He taught Vancouver's detectives that because glass could never be broken the same way twice, and because each piece of glass crystallizes in a slightly different way, finding even minuscule shards of glass at a crime scene could prove more valuable than fingerprints, which were often smudged beyond recognition or non-existent because criminals wore gloves or coated their hands with liquid latex.

At any one time, Vance had analyses of a dozen different police cases spread out over his lab. On June 15, 1933, he was brought the case of Joseph Hendrickson, an eighteen-year-old who had been shot in the

Vance in his lab, c.1932. *Courtesy of the Vance family*

head by a Chinese shopkeeper in a robbery that went horribly wrong.

Vance had been called out early that morning to visit the crime scene, a grocery store on the corner of Denman and Davie Streets at English Bay in Vancouver's West End. Constable George Gregson was first on the scene at 4:00 in the morning; he'd found Hendrickson lying on the sidewalk, an unoccupied DeSoto coupe parked with its engine running and headlights on, and an hysterical store employee named Goon Hing holding a shotgun. Constable Gregson dashed four stores down to the Princess Pat Tea Rooms and had the night man phone for an ambulance. The teenaged robber was taken to Vancouver General Hospital where he died the next day.

Goon Hing was arrested and charged with shooting with intent to do grievous bodily harm. At the police station, he told an interpreter named Gordon Cumyow[7] that he had only meant to scare the robbers. Hing told police that he and four other employees were asleep in a balcony at the back of the building. A noise woke him up, and when he came into the shop he saw someone crawling into the store through the front window. "I shouted 'Get away, stop' and awoke the others. The man remained in the store, and I shouted several more times for him to go away. When I saw him reach his right hand to his back pocket, I grabbed the shotgun hoping that I would frighten him away. When I fired, the two men disappeared, and I ducked behind the partition as I was afraid they might shoot. I did not see the man drop." The owner of the grocery store, Chan Yuen, phoned police. Goon Hing also told police that the gun belonged to his brother, a farmer, and he used it for hunting.

When Vance arrived, he took a look around the store, careful not to disturb the crime scene, and set about preserving the evidence as best he could. The front window had been smashed by gunshot pellets, and he could see where it had been jimmied and then propped open.

Detective Vince, Vance's assistant, took photos of the outside and inside of the store, paying special attention to the broken glass from the window, the bullet hole, the jimmy marks in the front window, the blood splatters on the door of the Frigidaire, and the footprints outside. There was a sack lying below the window that contained packets of Buckingham and British Consols cigarettes and a tin of Turrets cigarettes. Vance collected pellets from the shotgun and scraped away blood stains from an ice-cream container. He carefully gathered up a hair and pieces of glass from the shattered window, and then he took all

---

7   Gordon Cumyow was the son of Alexander Cumyow, the first Chinese person to be born in British Columbia, a community leader, and court interpreter. After he retired in 1936, Gordon took over as court interpreter, and in 1951 became the first Chinese notary in BC.

the specimens back to the lab for analysis. The evidence would either make a criminal case for the prosecution or confirm the shopkeeper's story of self defence.

First Vance confirmed that the stains were human blood and belonged to the same blood group as Hendrickson. Next he analyzed the hair and confirmed that it also belonged to Hendrickson. Taking several pieces of glass from the boy's sweater, he compared this to the broken glass from the window. If the trace from Hendrickson's sweater was the same as that found at the crime scene, the same spectrum bands would glow on the refractor. They matched perfectly. Criminals, he said, didn't realize that every contact left a trace.[8] When they smashed a window in the course of a robbery, they couldn't help but be showered with small particles of the material that would cling to their clothes.

It didn't take police long to pick up William Waugh, a cabinet maker and a friend of Hendrickson's, as the man who had driven the stolen car to the store to steal cigarettes. Waugh still had small fragments of glass clinging to his clothes, which were identical to those from the store window.

His statement to police also confirmed the evidence. "I stood alongside [Hendrickson] waiting for him to hand me some more cigarettes and then I heard this roar inside the store. I got frightened and I turned around and ran," Waugh told police. "Joe was knocked off his feet. He was blown right out."

At the inquest a few days later, the coroner's jury's decision was "death by misadventure."

In 1933, Police Chief Charles Edgett, the man who had seen the value in Vance's work and elevated him to the head of the newly formed

---

8 Edmond Locard—known as the Sherlock Holmes of France—opened the first dedicated forensic laboratory in 1910. The phrase "Every contact leaves a trace" is known as Locard's exchange principle.

By 1932 the media treated Vance as a celebrity, and he was frequently featured in articles such as this one in the *Province*, September 4, 1932. *Courtesy of the Vance family*

Police Bureau of Science, was fired for supposed inefficiency. Edgett was replaced by John Cameron, who as a young constable had enjoyed a distinguished career with the VPD. Cameron lost an eye to the job in 1917 when it was shot out in a gun battle with a drug dealer, which also claimed the life of his boss, Chief Malcolm MacLennan. Cameron had risen up the ranks and left the VPD in 1929 to take on the top job at New Westminster. When the VPD found itself with another vacancy, Mayor L.D. Taylor saw someone he could work with in Cameron. The chief knew his days were numbered in New Westminster, so he sold his majestic 4,000-square-foot Georgian mansion and moved back into the city and into an equally splendid house on a large corner block in Shaughnessy. Cameron would be the tenth police chief to serve during Vance's career, and one who experienced the VPD's well-earned reputation as "the graveyard of police chiefs." Cameron was intrigued

In the 1930s, Vance and his work were frequently featured in the national print media. *Ottawa Journal*, September 8, 1934. *Courtesy of the Vance family*

by Vance's invention, the "mechanical bloodhound," and renamed it the "Vancamoscope," a combination of the names of its inventor and new benefactor.

POISON

It was 10:00 p.m. on April 13, 1933, and nineteen-year-old Stewart Ashley had just finished his regular workout at the YMCA. Glen Nixon, who worked there, offered him a ride home if he could wait twenty minutes, but Stewart politely declined and started to walk toward Cambie and Hastings Streets where he would normally catch the streetcar home. When Ashley failed to arrive home that night, his family became concerned, and when he was still not home by the next morning, they called police.

Young men went missing all the time, and the police took little notice until two days later when the Ashleys received a ransom note in the Saturday mail. The note arrived on plain paper enclosed in a plain envelope. The message and the address on the envelope were typed. The note was short and to the point: "Get $5,000 by April 20 or your son will die. You will hear again on the 19th."

In 1933, the Depression was at its height. One out of five Canadians was dependent on some form of government relief, while thirty percent of the labour force was unemployed. In British Columbia—where the average income for those who still had a job was $777—$5,000 was a huge amount of money.[9] And while a missing boy wasn't news, a kidnapped one quickly made the front page of all the daily newspapers.

Vance's own two sons, Jack and Tom, were close in age to Stewart, and like everyone else in the city, he closely followed the kidnapping story

---

9 The average ranged from $353 to $1,600. See Statistics Canada: http://www65.statcan.gc.ca/acyb02/1947/acyb02_19470552021-eng.htm and https://thetyee.ca/Views/2008/11/26/BCDepression/

in the newspapers. Vance wasn't initially involved in the investigation into Stewart's disappearance, but he stayed in the loop through his police colleagues. He hoped that the young man would be found quickly. On April 18, the day before the next set of ransom instructions were due, Stewart's father, David Ashley, gave an interview to the *Vancouver Sun*. When the reporter asked him what he would do if his son was not found before the deadline, Ashley told the reporter that he hadn't decided. "I am guided by the advice of Chief John Cameron in this matter," he said. "In any case, $5,000 is a great deal of money, and for a man of my means it would be very difficult to raise it."

The date when the promised second note was to be delivered to the Ashleys came and went. And with no new sightings, no leads, and no follow-up, the newspapers moved onto other headlines. The question that wasn't asked was: who would want to kidnap Stewart Ashley?

A newly minted teacher, fresh out of a two-year program at the University of BC, he'd been taking a few courses at the Provincial Normal School and getting the odd job as a substitute teacher. Stewart was six feet (183 cm) tall and of medium build with dark hair, dark eyes, and a dark complexion. The newspaper photographs show a good-looking, serious young man. He was described as a "young man of scholarly habits, who did not drink or frequent places of amusement and displayed little interest in women." He liked crosswords, jigsaws, badminton, skating, and reading. Except for his twice-weekly gym sessions, he rarely went out, and if he did go to a dance, it was to take one of his sisters.

His older sister Irma told a reporter: "He was very fond of studying and reading, and latterly about the only evenings when he was not with us were Monday and Thursday when he attended gym class at the YWCA. He had absolutely no reason for wanting to go away."

Stewart lived with his parents and sisters. His father worked as a notary, and police told reporters that they thought David Ashley may have been targeted for the ransom because of his job. Although not wealthy, criminals may have thought he could come up with the money. David Ashley said that the last time he saw his son was on April 13 when Stewart was leaving for the gym. He had about five dollars on him, and he hadn't noticed anything unusual about his manner. In fact, he was perfectly normal and reasonable and had no troubles of any kind, said his father. Stewart kept regular hours and never gave his parents cause for concern. And while he wasn't yet getting regular work as a substitute teacher, he didn't think his son had financial worries.

Stewart Ashley, his sister Irma, and a sample of his handwriting. *Daily Province*, April 26, 1933. *Courtesy of the Vance family*

Investigators questioned his former school mates. They told him that in high school Stewart was regarded as "unusual." He kept to himself and didn't join in on typical high school pranks. At UBC, his fellow students told police a similar story. Stewart was aloof, they said. He made few friends, and although he wasn't disliked, he wasn't particularly well-liked either.

Around 7:00 p.m. on Sunday, April 23—exactly ten days after Stewart

Nineteen-year-old Stewart Ashley. *Vancouver Sun*, April 24, 1933. *Courtesy of the Vance family*

went missing—twelve-year-old Richard Tisdale and his younger brother Herbert were playing in the old Songhees Reserve near Victoria on Vancouver Island. Herbert was throwing stones into a scum-covered pond at the bottom of a steep embankment when he noticed a body floating face-down in the water below. The boys ran to get help.

Constable Harry Mercer was the first police officer to arrive at the scene. He found the body of a young man lying in about two feet (sixty-one cm) of stagnant water. The body, which was quickly identified as Stewart Ashley, was clean-shaven and dressed in a dark blue suit. On one hand he wore a glove which covered two rings; one bore his initials, S.A., the other the initials P.N.S.—the Provincial Normal School. Police found two clean handkerchiefs in Stewart's suit pocket. There was also a Vancouver streetcar pass and a newspaper clipping from November 1932. Pencilled on the clipping was a telephone number, B607R (Bayview 607-R), which turned out to be that of his aunt Helen Cathcart, who lived in Vancouver.

Constables Mercer, Perris Atkinson, and Douglas Bone pulled on rubber boots, stripped to the waist, and began to drag the muddy bottom of the pond looking for the missing glove, a piece of material torn from the knee of Stewart's pants, and any other evidence they may have missed. After about an hour, Constable Mercer dragged up a bundle weighted down by a fifteen-pound (seven-kg) rock, tied with a heavy cord. Inside was a grey tweed cap, a white gym sweater, and a pair of grey pants with a laundry tag on the waistband numbered 416062R.

The police investigation centred around the clothes and the ransom note. Why wasn't a second note sent, and why there was no attempt to collect the money? Detectives speculated to reporters that the kidnappers may have lost their nerve and killed Stewart. Chief Cameron told reporters: "We're sure of just one thing now, and that is that he was dead when he went into that slough.

Photos of the pond near Victoria where Stewart Ashley's body was found. *Daily Colonist*, April 25, 1933. *Courtesy of the Vance family*

His lungs were as dry as my finger, and no man can go alive into a pool of water, injured or uninjured, without taking some water at least into his lungs."

Cameron, Inspector McLeod, and Inspector Vance came from Vancouver to work with Victoria's Police Chief Thomas Heatley and Detective Inspector Jack McLellan. They were joined by Staff Sergeants Rodger Peachey and W.A. MacBrayne of the Provincial Police, and they had the full force of their police departments behind them.

Vance went straight to the pond where Stewart's body was found. He spent some time examining the crime scene and then gathered clay from the water's edge and soil from the top of the embankment, which he noted was twenty-four feet (seven meters) above the slough and had a steep incline.

While Victoria police followed the few leads available, Vance returned to Vancouver to examine the dead man's stomach contents, liver, and intestines and determine the cause of death. Vance suspected poison. Poison, he said, was so subtle that it would not necessarily be detected in the post-mortem examination. He refused to be rushed. It might take a few hours, he told reporters, it might take a few days. There are more than 600 poisons that could kill a person, but Vance felt the poison that had killed Stewart was likely one of a dozen. Vance methodically followed a process of elimination. After a few days of lab analysis, there was no doubt in his mind that Stewart had died quickly from cyanide poisoning.

While Vance was determining cause of death, Vancouver police were trying to solve the mystery surrounding the clothes that Stewart had worn when he died. The Ashley family told police that they didn't recognize the clothes, but police found a laundry number on a coat in Stewart's closet that matched that on his pants. This led them to Connaught Cleaners and Dryers on West Broadway, where the owner, Earl Fitzpatrick, identified the numbered tag on Stewart's pants. Fitzgerald said that the number "41" represented the cleaner's plant number and "6062" identified Stewart as the customer. The suit had been dropped off for cleaning a year earlier. The pants were part of a golf ensemble, he said, which consisted of a coat, vest, shorts, and trousers. Police found the rest of the suit at the Ashley home, and one of the photographs that the family had given to the media showed Stewart wearing the short pants.

Police stepped up their efforts to find a timeline for Stewart's movements from the moment he went missing on April 13 to the time that he went into the pond ten days later. Police gave the media a sample of his handwriting and asked that every rooming house and hotel check their registry to see if there was a match. There were no reported sightings of Stewart on the boats to Victoria, and no one knew when or how he had got to Vancouver Island. The mystery of his movements fuelled speculation about the kidnapping, although no one could seem to account for the fact that he had recently shaved and was wearing a nice suit.

The mystery of Stewart Ashley's disappearance and death. *Vancouver Sun*, April 27, 1933. *Courtesy of the Vance family*

His shoes showed little wear, which indicated that he hadn't walked very far in them.

Newspaper stories raised the question about how his body got into the slough. Had he been thrown from a train or dumped from a car on the highway? There were no bruises on his body, which made both scenarios unlikely.

When it was suggested that death might have been caused by carbon monoxide from the exhaust of a gasoline-propelled engine, the papers jumped on this theory. Had Stewart been lured to a boat somewhere on the Vancouver waterfront, held prisoner, and asphyxiated while on board? The theory would explain why he hadn't been seen on any boat from Vancouver. Although unproven, one paper ran the headline "Killed by Gas on Kidnapper's Boat."

But the next day, Chief Cameron announced that they were no

longer pursuing the kidnapping theory. Stewart had been seen near Ladysmith on Vancouver Island north of Victoria around noon on April 20, and in Victoria on April 21. Both times he was seen travelling alone. Ladysmith resident Annie Provis told police that she saw a young man of Stewart's description walking along the railway tracks and they had a brief conversation about the weather. "I came face to face with this young man. The sun was shining on his face," she told police. "He seemed surprised to see me, and then he spoke to me and said, 'What a beautiful day.' He did not laugh; he looked quite troubled." Provis said he was wearing a dark suit with a vest and a white shirt. "His clothes were very dusty, and he was carrying a small bundle," she said.

When Allan MacLachlan, an engineer with the Esquimalt and Nanaimo Railway, read that a body had been found in the slough and then saw Stewart's photograph, he was sure it was the same young man he had seen board the engine tender on his passenger train at Nanaimo on Friday, April 21. He noticed Stewart, he said, because he was well-dressed, wearing a blue suit with a white shirt and grey cap—not the usual "hobo" trying to hitch a ride on the train. MacLachlan said he saw Stewart at Nanaimo and again at Goldstream near Victoria, when the train stopped for water. At the undertakers in Vancouver's Mount Pleasant neighbourhood, MacLachlan positively identified the body as that of the young man who had looked so out of place on the train.

Archibald Sturrock, a master mechanic on the same railway, also identified Stewart from his photo in the paper. He said that he'd ordered Stewart off the train at Russell Station in Victoria at 10:40 in the morning on Saturday, April 22, because he'd been sitting in a dangerous spot. Sturrock said he noticed him because he was travelling alone. "'You are too nice a boy,' I said to him. 'You will get into trouble.'

This boy had a very depressed look. The queer part of it was, when I spoke to him, he did not answer." Stewart stayed at the station when the train moved away, said Sturrock.

The police investigation then focussed on the typed ransom note, and this led them to the Provincial Normal School. Helmi Doidge, who worked in the office, told them that she had seen Stewart in the office about ten days before his disappearance and that he would have had access to the school's typewriter that was in her office, the only one in the school. Henry B. MacLean,[10] an expert on handwriting and typewriting, examined the ransom note and confirmed that the letters were the same as those typed on the "noiseless typewriter" in Doidge's office. The face of the type on a noiseless machine, he said, is different from other machines. MacLean believed the typing had been done by a person who wasn't used to working on one of these kinds of typewriters and pointed to a typo where the word "son" had been typed as "sob." "The 'b' and the 'n' are close together," he said.

The next day, the *Vancouver Sun* did an about-face with the front-page headline: "Ashley Not Kidnapped Declares Police Chief." But as the cause of death had not yet been released, reporters returned to the family for news. Elva, Stewart's younger sister, told a reporter: "There has been a lot of talk that Stewart went away of his own accord. Surely he is exonerated by what has happened. Surely no one could believe that he would leave us without a word." Added Irma, Stewart's older sister: "I am sure that Stewart never went away of his own accord. It is unthinkable, we were so close to one another." Elva had been away, she said, and Stewart was to meet her on Easter Friday, the day after his disappearance. "Stewart and Elva were constantly together," said

---

10 Generations of Canadian school children learned the "whole arm" or "muscular movement" method of handwriting from *The MacLean Method of Writing* (Vancouver: Clarke & Stuart, 1921).

A bench in the lab where Vance tested for blood and examined organs for poisons.
Courtesy of the Vance family

Irma. "And I can never believe that he would have run away on the very night that he was supposed to meet her."

On Thursday, May 4, the inquiry into Stewart Ashley's death was held in front of a coroner's jury of six randomly selected men. Vance walked the jury through Stewart's last actions. "I could follow his every movement from the specimens of soil I obtained from the scene of the tragedy," he told them.

Stewart had taken the rock, tied it to his bundle of extra clothing, and thrown it into the pool. Then he sat down on the bank. Vance knew this, he said, because the dirt he found on the seat of Stewart's pants and the tail of his coat was the same as that found at the top of the bank. There was no evidence that anyone was with him. Stewart then swallowed the cyanide that he had brought with him. The poison would almost immediately cause paralysis of the lungs and create muscular convulsions, causing Stewart to roll over and down the bank.

The clay and mud stains on Stewart's clothing matched the soil on the bank and weren't ground into the clothing as heavily as the stains on the trouser seat or coat tails. The grass and crushed vegetation at the top of the bank had been thrown forward, indicating the body had rolled and stopped face-down in the slough. The bank

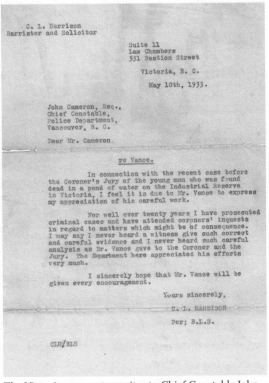

C. L. Harrison
Barrister and Solicitor

Suite 11
Law Chambers
531 Bastion Street

Victoria, B. C.

May 10th, 1933.

John Cameron, Esq.,
Chief Constable,
Police Department,
Vancouver, B. C.

Dear Mr. Cameron,

re Vance.

In connection with the recent case before the Coroner's Jury of the young man who was found dead in a pond of water on the Industrial Reserve in Victoria, I feel it is due to Mr. Vance to express my appreciation of his careful work.

For well over twenty years I have prosecuted criminal cases and have attended coroners' inquests in regard to matters which might be of consequence. I may say I never heard a witness give such correct and careful evidence and I never heard such careful analysis as Dr. Vance gave to the Coroner and the Jury. The Department here appreciated his efforts very much.

I sincerely hope that Mr. Vance will be given every encouragement.

Yours sincerely,

C. L. HARRISON

Per; B.L.S.

CLH/BLS

The Victoria prosecutor writes to Chief Constable John Cameron commending Vance on his work in the Stewart Ashley case. *Courtesy of the Vance family*

had a sixty percent incline, which would have facilitated the body's descent. Cyanide typically worked within two to three minutes, but because Stewart had eaten peanuts shortly before he took the poison, the acidity caused by the oils in the peanuts would have made death much quicker. Stewart, said Vance, was dead before he hit the water. Vance explained that the Provincial Normal School, where Stewart attended classes, kept potassium cyanide in the nature study classroom for killing insects. The room was not locked, and Stewart would have been able to access it there. It was also used in photography and mining and could be purchased in most drugstores.

"The condition is so plain—where he went, where he stood, where his feet went, and where he rolled down," Vance told the coroner's jury. "It is so distinct. I have never seen anything so plain." Based on the scientific evidence presented, it was his opinion that Stewart sat on the edge of the slough, swallowed the cyanide pill, and then fell into the pond.

It was a straightforward reconstruction of the death—to everyone, it seemed, except the coroner's jury. The verdict was that Stewart Ashley came to his death on or about April 22 "from the effects of poison, that is to say, potassium cyanide, and that we do not consider there is sufficient evidence to decide as to when, how, where, or by whom it was administered." It was a disappointing but perhaps not surprising verdict. Several questions remained unanswered: Where was Stewart from the time he went missing on April 13 until his conversation with Annie Provis just outside Nanaimo seven days later? How did he get to Vancouver Island, and why did no one see him? Where did he get the shoes and why didn't they show wear? And, most baffling at all, why would he send a note to his father asking for the ridiculous sum of $5,000?

When I asked David Klonsky, an associate professor in the psychology department at the University of BC who specializes in suicide, for a modern-day explanation for Stewart's death, he told me that pain and hopelessness are the main motivations for people who attempt suicide. Stewart was very close to his sisters, and one theory could be that one or both had boyfriends and were thinking of starting their own families, which could have meant to Stewart the end of his close relationships with them and therefore of his own very limited social life. The newspapers referred to his inability to form friendships with his school friends and his disinterest in women.

It is possible to surmise that Stewart was gay and was unable to come out to his family. In the 1930s, homosexuality was illegal. Ron

Dutton, archivist for the BC Gay and Lesbian Archives, told me that most people in Vancouver in that era would have hidden their sexuality. "To be out was to be ostracized socially. You'd lose your job, you'd lose your family, you'd lose your place in the community, and you would be identified as an easy target for violence. Many gay people lived permanently closeted lives."

Klonsky says that people sometimes use self-harm as a way to lash out or for revenge, and the ransom note and subsequent suicide could have been a way to hurt his father. On the other hand, Klonsky suggests that Stewart could have been in serious debt. "Perhaps he felt estranged from his family and his community. Maybe he just wanted to go somewhere else and he needed money for that, and he saw this as a potential way out. But then he didn't get it, and that was his last hope," says Klonsky.

Stewart may not have made many friends in life, but all the media attention turned him into a celebrity, and 350 people attended his funeral.

On May 8, 1933, Victoria's Chief Heatley wrote to Vance: "Although the verdict of the Coroner's Jury was disappointing and left a certain degree of doubt in the minds of some, no one who was present at the inquest and heard the evidence adduced by yourself could possibly entertain the slightest doubt as to the manner and cause of the young man's death."

The Vancouver Police Department Annual Report for 1933 gave Vance and the Police Bureau of Science credit for securing convictions for eighty-four major criminal cases that year, including solving much of the mystery surrounding Stewart Ashley's death. Inspector Vance's unique services, noted Chief Cameron in the report, were much in demand outside Vancouver.

Second letter sent to Vance on March 2, 1934, warning him to keep away from Stitton and Woolf's upcoming trial. Courtesy of the Vance family

LAY OFF, OR WE'LL BUMP YOU OFF!

The letter arrived at Inspector Vance's lab on February 13, 1934. It was crudely printed on a sheet of dirty paper: "Lay off or we'll bump you off!" The rest of the message was indecipherable. Vance phoned Deputy Chief John Murdoch, who told him that police officers often received such letters and that he shouldn't worry. Vance filed the letter away in his drawer. A phone call followed: "Lay off, Vance, or your life ain't worth a dime," said a male voice before hanging up.

On March 5, a second threatening letter addressed to Vance arrived at the police station's general office. This one said, "Keep away from Stirton's trial." Vance wrote in his notebook: "The letter had filthy language and asked that I wear a flower if I intended to remain away [from the courtroom]."

Vance showed the second threatening letter to Murdoch. Again he was told not to worry.

Cunningham Drug Store would eventually become part of Shoppers Drug Mart, but in 1934 it was a chain of twelve stores owned by a former Woodward's department store pharmacist named George Cunningham. In the early hours of Sunday morning, January 7, the store in the Vancouver Block on Granville Street was robbed of cash and drugs. The robbery was discovered at 4:30 a.m., and within a couple of hours, police had suspects firmly in their sights: a career criminal named George Stirton and Reginald Woolf, a taxi driver. Woolf had rented a car from the Moonlight U-Drive, which was later seen outside the drugstore at the time of the robbery. A few hours later, it was found parked in the lane behind Stirton's West End apartment and quickly traced to Woolf.

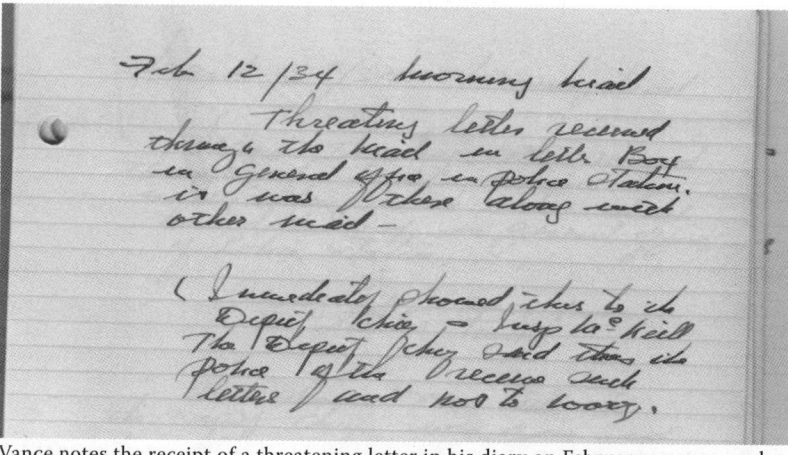

Vance notes the receipt of a threatening letter in his diary on February 12, 1934, and the deputy chief's response that police often received such letters and "not to worry." *Courtesy of the Vance family*

Stirton had been released from Oakalla Prison Farm two months before, where he'd served an eighteen-month sentence for possession of nitroglycerin. When police raided his Burnaby Street apartment, they found a bag of burglar's tools in the garden, a wrecking bar on a fence ledge outside his door, and inside, a steel punch and a key that fit the basement entrance to the Vancouver Block. They also found nitroglycerin, morphine, cocaine, and a bottle of Vaseline hair tonic, all taken from the drugstore.

Crimes against property peaked during the Depression years in Vancouver. Before credit cards and debit transactions, most businesses kept a safe on the premises to secure the day's take in cash. Safecrackers, or "yeggs" as they were known, were skilled in the use of highly dangerous explosives; nitroglycerin, known as "soup," was the favoured method. Just a drop of the pure fluid could blow off a hand, and a small jar's worth was enough to set off an explosion that would crack a safe. Several times during his career, Vance was called to a safecracking that had gone wrong and asked to neutralize the explosives.

Vance testified at Stirton and Woolf's preliminary hearing on

INSPECTOR J. F. C. B. VANCE, police scientist, was called out this morning to "de-soup" this vault in UBC administration building, after yeggs had made at least four unsuccessful attempts to open it.

Vance is called in to "de-soup" a safe in 1947 after attempts to crack it went awry. *Daily Province,* April 9, 1947. *Courtesy of the Vance family*

January 29, and they knew that it would be Vance's scientific evidence at the upcoming trial that would put them away.

The day after the second threatening letter arrived, the doorbell to Vance's lab rang. There was no one there, but he could see a man running down the stairs. Others reported seeing unknown men hanging around the hallway.

The following day, Vance ignored the advice from the Deputy Chief and began to worry.

On Wednesday, March 7, Vance collected his mail from the general office and took it back to his lab. He put aside some letters, picked up a bulky-looking parcel, and started to untie the string. He happened to glance at the printed address. The bad handwriting immediately reminded him of the writing on the warning letters that he'd received. He called in Detectives Vince and Anderson who were both assigned to work in the Police Bureau of Science.

Then, with his customary patience, he slowly removed the string and unwrapped the package. Inside was a small box used to hold handkerchiefs that contained a crude but effective homemade bomb. Two wires and a detonator were fixed in such a way that if the string

Vance narrowly escaped death after receiving this home-made bomb through the mail in March 1934. *Courtesy of the Vance family*

had been broken or jerked, the bomb would have exploded, killing Vance and taking out a significant chunk of the building, and many of the people in it. Detective Vince traced the cardboard handkerchief box to Cunningham Drug Store. Chief Cameron ordered that Vance be placed under guard at work and at home while the spring assize court was in session.

While Vance was fending off attempts on his life and working on several other cases, strange things began to happen in and around the police station. The day after the mail bomb incident, David Quigley, the morgue attendant, was on his way to the lab to talk to Vance when he noticed two suspicious men—one tall and one short—loitering on the landing. He recognized the short man as a taxi driver who worked from a stand at the corner of Granville and Helmcken Streets. Later that afternoon, Quigley received a phone call at the morgue telling him to watch his step and to "lay off." The call was traced to a public pay phone.

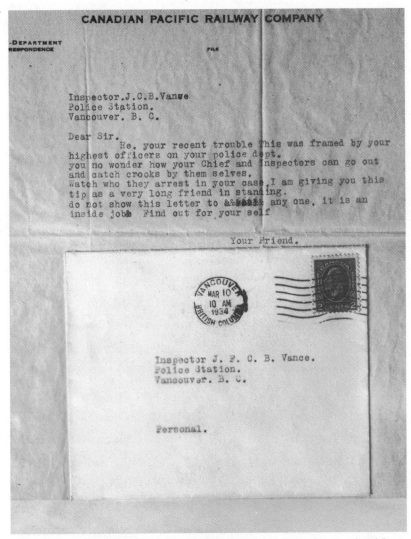

CANADIAN PACIFIC RAILWAY COMPANY

-DEPARTMENT
RESPONDENCE   FILE

Inspector.J.C.B.Vance
Police Station.
Vancouver. B. C.

Dear Sir.
        Re. your recent trouble This was framed by your
highest officers on your police dept.
you no wonder how your Chief and Inspectors can go out
and catch crooks by them selves.
Watch who they arrest in your case,I am giving you this
tip as a very long friend in standing.
do not show this letter to ɑ̶t̶ any one, it is an
inside job. Find out for your self

                                    Your Friend.

VANCOUVER
MAR 10
10 AM
1934
BRITISH COLUMBIA

Inspector J. F. C. B. Vance.
Police Station.
Vancouver. B. C.

Personal.

Vance receives an anonymous letter on CPR letterhead warning of an "inside job."
Courtesy of the Vance family

Meanwhile, Detective Vince's wife Emily was bowling with her team at the LaSalle Bowling Alley on Granville Street when Harvey Halliday, a local thug, approached her and asked, "What does your old man do?" Mrs Vince, a former telephone operator at the police station, told him her husband was the "fingerprint man." "He had better not take my fingerprints," Halliday told her, then asked what Vance did. "He's the Bureau of Science man," she said. "He's a dirty bastard," Halliday responded, saying, "He's going to get something he does not want." What Vince hadn't told his anxious wife was that he'd noticed a strange man watching their home and walking up and down the block where they lived. Halliday, who was already facing a charge of intimidating a witness, was picked up and taken in for questioning on suspicion of having sent the bomb to Vance's lab. He was later released for lack of evidence.

Chief Cameron requested funds to install two iron grilles at the top of the stairway leading to Vance's lab on the upper floors of the building. The doors were locked at 6:00 p.m. and opened again at 7:00 a.m., so no one could enter during those hours without a key. "Mr Vance frequently works in the laboratory late at night and fears are entertained that underworld characters who already have forwarded one deadly bomb through the mails to the inspector may even go to the extent of bombing the laboratory," the chief told the budget-conscious police commission. He pointed out that the grilles would provide extra security for the court exhibits as well as important documents in the prosecutor's office.

The second attempt on Vance's life came less than a week later, on Sunday, March 11, and this time it struck close to home. At around 10:00 p.m., Constable Duncan Fraser was on duty at the Vance house when he heard an odd sound coming from the back of the house and went out to investigate. He couldn't see anyone but heard the sound of running footsteps. He ran to the front of the house just in time to see a man disappear into the thick bush of an adjoining lot. When he checked the basement, he saw one of the windows had been tampered with. There was nothing taken or placed inside, but the incident put police on high alert. Vance was given a police driver and bodyguard, and another police guard was placed on duty at his house.

Shortly before midnight on the following Friday night, Detective Leonard Parsons was patrolling the grounds of the Vance residence when he noticed the distinctive smell of burning powder coming from the back of the house. There he saw a red glow under the window of Vance's home office. The quick-thinking detective ran over to the burning fuse, whipped out his pocket knife, and cut off the end. The fuse hissed for a few seconds and died. Throwing a beam from his flashlight, he saw that he was holding a piece of burned-out fuse about the length of his arm. A shorter piece was still attached to a tin can containing black powder and rags that was buried under the house.

The Cunningham Drug Store robbery trial started on March 19. Newspaper headlines such as "Vance Escapes Bomb Plot," and "Death Parcel for Scientist," had made him a celebrity, and the courtroom was packed with people wanting to see how scientific evidence would help to convict the safecrackers. City detectives and uniformed police officers spread out to keep the crowd under close surveillance. Vance entered the court with a police escort, and when he wasn't giving evidence, he sat flanked between Detectives William Grant and Harry Duggan.

Vance explained that he'd been called to the crime scene at 10:00 on the morning of the robbery. He found the store littered with wet towels and coats which were used to deaden the noise of the explosion.

Constable William Davidson of the Provincial Police wheeled over the first exhibit—the door of the drugstore's safe. Vance demonstrated the use of nitroglycerin in safe-blowing, and showed the jury how a homemade dial puller, found the day of the theft near Stirton's West End apartment, had been used on the safe door and how the screw-bolts of the puller fitted into the marks on the door.

Vance moved between the witness stand and the jury to demonstrate the use of various items.

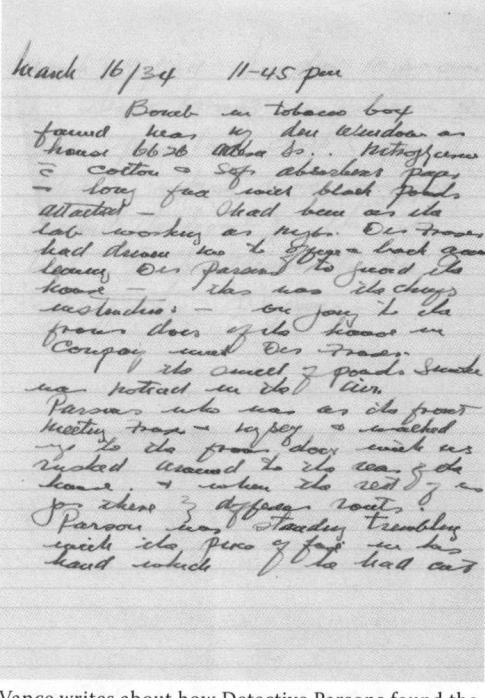

Vance writes about how Detective Parsons found the bomb under a window in his house on Adera Street in March 1934. *Courtesy of the Vance family*

He told the jury that the safe's brass dial had been pried off with a chisel and a screwdriver. He took out a large magnifying glass and invited the jury to examine the piles of earth, flakes of mica, a fragment of brass, and smears of paint on the door and dial of the safe as he reconstructed the robbery for them. Under the magnifying glass, Vance showed them how a tiny piece of brass found in Stirton's handkerchief fit into the safe's dial, which had been chiselled open. He showed them that the screwdriver found at Stirton's home still had a small flake of the brass attached. Vance then produced some flakes of red paint from a sealed envelope. These, he told the jury, he had scraped from the right knee of Stirton's pants. The paint was identical to that found on the dial puller.

Among the exhibits were a bundle of rags, a pair of shoes, and two pairs of gloves, which Vance found in a small hole behind a toilet in Stirton's apartment. The items were wet when he found them, and the shoes and one rag bore traces of mica. From other envelopes he produced flakes of mica found in the drugstore and similar flakes taken from the cuffs of the trousers of Stirton and Woolf when arrested.

One of the biggest exhibits, next to the safe door, was an automobile seat taken from the rented car that police believed was used by the safecrackers. Vance told the jury that he'd found cinders and ash on the car seat. The fusion of these ashes was unusual, he said, and were the same as those found at the rear of the store. Vance produced pieces of the burned fuse found in the drugstore as well as two similar pieces, with live detonators attached, which police had found in a hedge alongside Stirton's home.

Stirton's lawyer told the jury that either his client was framed or he was the dumbest client ever for leaving all the evidence lying around. It failed to sway them. The jury deliberated for ten minutes before bringing back a guilty verdict.

Outside, a crowd stood watching as the two prisoners, handcuffed and under heavy police escort, walked out of the cells to the waiting patrol wagon. Several women and a few male friends waved goodbye as the wagon moved off on its way to Oakalla Prison Farm. Stirton was sentenced to eight years for breaking and entering the Cunningham Drug Store, two years for having explosives, and another six months for having drugs in his possession. Woolf received five years.

"It was a triumph for Vance, who was the crown's key witness—but it may be a triumph gained at the expense of the health and peace of mind of the Vancouver criminologist," wrote a reporter. "Vance, now under constant police guard, is feeling the nervous strain and it is noticeable in his appearance." But at the end of the trial, Chief Cameron believed that the threat to Vance was over, and he had the guards removed from Vance's house.

Then, on the evening of April 22, 1934, there was another attempt on his life.

Vance and his family were returning from church when he turned into their driveway and his car's headlights caught a man running across their yard toward the lane and disappearing over the back fence.

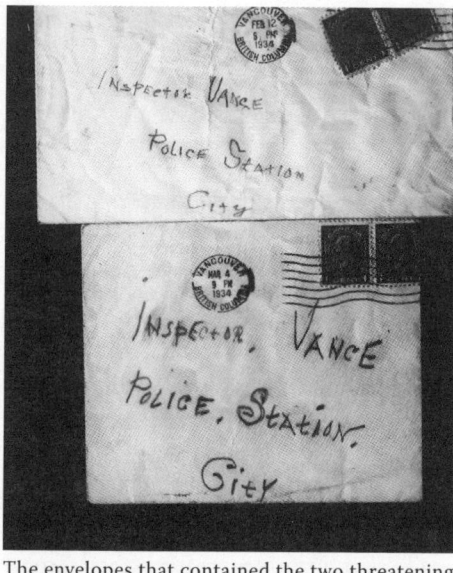

The envelopes that contained the two threatening letters sent to Vance. *Courtesy of the Vance family*

When Vance went inside to call police, he found that the telephone was dead. Young Tom Vance was sent to the neighbour's house to use their phone, and when police arrived they found the wires leading into the house had been cut and a basement window forced open. Police told Vance they thought it was the work of burglars trying to break into the house.

Stirton and Woolf weren't the only criminals that Vance had to worry about. He was also due to give evidence in two major trials that were receiving front-page headlines—the shooting of a Vancouver crime boss and a hit-and-run being tried as a murder.

One Tuesday night in December 1933, Josie Celona turned up drunk at her ex-husband's Point Grey house. There, she took an axe to their locked door. Joe Celona, a notorious brothel owner, was in bed with another woman. Josie fired off a couple of shots as the fleeing couple jumped out of the bedroom window. When Dorothy Yamada, the Celonas' maid, phoned police, Josie grabbed the phone and told them: "I have shot my husband so you had better do something about it. You will see his guts lying outside." When Constable W.C. York arrived, Josie pointed to a small automatic pistol lying on the kitchen table and said: "I have thrown it down and stamped on it, and it won't go off any more." York found a live bullet jammed in the chamber and three others in the magazine.

"You bastards are the cause of all my trouble," she told Constable York.

York left her in the house and went looking for the wounded husband. He found Joe a few blocks away shoving the other woman into a cab. Joe told him that he had not been shot and returned to the house with the officer. Back at the house, Josie swore, spat, and tried to kick her former husband, then threw a lit cigarette in his face.

Josie was charged with shooting with intent to kill. A few hours later, police found Joe being attended to for a gunshot wound by Dr Maurice Fox at a room in the Maple Hotel where Joe operated a brothel. Joe told the detective that he had accidentally shot himself in the arm and the bullet had gone through his arm and his belt and into his side.

The next day, police gathered up the clothes Joe had been wearing, the gun, the badly smashed bedroom door, a glass door knob, and an axe, and took them to Vance's lab. At the trial, Vance drew the court's attention to the hole through the belt and the waistband of Joe's trousers and another through the shirt and the underclothing. He found blood around the holes, he said, but no powder burns, which indicated the gun had not been fired at close range. Vance believed that Josie had shot him after all, despite his claims.

Josie, who the newspapers said wore a smart black spring hat and squirrel-trimmed seal jacket, was found guilty and sentenced to the time she had already spent in jail—it amounted to less than a day.

The following day, Vance was back in court giving evidence about a hit-and-run.

On October 13, 1933, Bryce Boyd, a thirty-year-old marine engineer, had spent the day drinking with his buddy, a sailor named Percy Conover. Later that evening, they met up with Violet York, whose longshoreman husband had been back in England for the past year, and her friend Emily Pearson. The four finished the night off at Blackie's, a bootlegging joint on East Hastings Street. As they were stumbling out around 2:00 a.m., four husky Scandinavian loggers walked by and asked them what was going on inside. Boyd gave them an answer that would change his life: "None of your business." The next minute, he and Conover were on the losing end of an unmatched fight. The women managed to get the two men into Violet's car, putting Boyd in the driver's seat, and they took off after the four loggers. Boyd drove up over the sidewalk and slammed into Karl Nordberg, catching him behind the knees with the bumper, then dragging him down the street. One of the other loggers, all of whom had been drinking heavily that day, was hit in the side. Nordberg was taken to hospital and died later from internal hemorrhaging.

Boyd managed to stay conscious long enough to drive the car to Violet's Kitsilano house. Within hours, the police had tracked the car to a garage nearby her house. It had a bent crank shaft and loose steering. Police found Boyd hiding in an attic at Violet's house, the entrance to which was gained through a trap door in the bathroom ceiling. Boyd was charged with the murder of Karl Nordberg. He told them that he had no recollection of hitting anyone. The others couldn't remember anything either, they said.

When Vance arrived at the crime scene, he started by searching for footprints. He noted the direction from which they'd come, the weight of the impressions, the length of the stride, and whether the impression was made by the full shoe or just the heel or the ball of the foot. When he was satisfied that he had found all of them, he covered the shoe impressions with empty boxes. Next he looked at the tire marks and marked the direction of the tracks by driving pegs into the ground. He noticed that the tire impressions in the soil were heavier at one spot, indicating that the car had stopped at that point. Vance then started a methodical search of the surrounding soil and vegetation. He paused from time to time to place samples in small glass containers and envelopes that he'd brought along for that purpose. Then he began to look for other trace evidence such as glass fragments, wood splinters, fabric, or human hair that could help the police investigation and ultimately build a case.

The car's bumper, two tires, a floor mat, wheel rim, and Nordberg's trousers had been sent to the lab for Vance to examine. Vance was able to fit a piece of cloth that he'd extracted from the front bumper of the car into a hole torn in the rear of Nordberg's trousers. He found blood stains on the seat, floor, and door handle of the car, which were not from Nordberg's blood group but could have come from either Boyd or Conover, who were both bleeding when they got into the car.

Moving to his microscope, Vance compared dirt found where the car went over the curb with dirt scraped from under the car. The same builder's waste material—containing sand, concrete, and pieces of red tile—was found in both samples. When he examined the left rear tire, Vance found the same dirt that he'd retrieved from the vacant lot where Nordberg had been hit.

When presented with these findings in court, there was now no doubt that the car Boyd had admitted to driving was the same one that killed Nordberg, said the judge. It was up to the jury to determine if Boyd's actions were murder or manslaughter, or whether he was not guilty. "Remember, there was a scuffle outside Blackie's and ... two men were overpowered by the other four in the presence of women with whom they had been going the rounds of beer parlours and bootleggers. If Boyd was so drunk that he didn't know what he was doing, then he had committed no crime, because that would be a form of insanity."

The jury agreed. Even though Vance's evidence had proved that, without a doubt, Boyd was behind the wheel of the car that killed Nordberg, the jury felt he had not been in his right mind. At the sentencing, the judge told Boyd: "I am free to say that you received what an ordinary young man, accompanying lady friends, would consider provocation. I am not inclined to take too serious a view of your case." Boyd promised that he would not drive again without permission from the chief of police, and he was sentenced to time already served.

As Vance's reputation grew, so did offers from other police departments around the world. Early in 1934, he was approached by a representative of the Chinese government with an offer to establish a crime detection laboratory in Asia. He was sorely tempted. He was often in the Vancouver lab for fifteen hours a day, and he spent many weekends there as well. When he'd applied for a salary increase, city aldermen raised a storm of protest, and the aldermen's protests usually made the newspapers. Suggestions that Vance be put on the provincial government payroll or that his lab become a consulting bureau for every police department that needed his services fell on deaf ears.

Vance requested that $100 a month for expenses be added to his salary, which had been slashed from $5,000 to $3,825 when all civic salaries were cut the year before. Vance was holding down three official positions but being paid for only one—and not paid well. In addition to being an Inspector of the VPD, he was still the city analyst and the morgue's toxicologist. His request for a salary increase was met with howls of outrage. While acknowledging the great work he was doing, his increased responsibilities, and the results he was getting, Mayor L.D. Taylor said that if Vance was allowed the increase, he would be making almost $100 more than Dr J.W. McIntosh, the Medical Health Officer, and $75 more than the chief of police. "I could not see why he needed $100 a month and extra equipment at this time," Taylor said. "I'm skeptical of the value of the work done by this department. Long before we had such a branch the police were obtaining convictions against criminals just the same as they are now."

Despite the Mayor's objections, however, $1,500 for new equipment was allocated. Moments later, Alderman DeGraves jumped to his feet when he discovered another item in the police budget estimates that provided $100 to Vance for two new suits. "This is too rich!" he said. Mayor Taylor quietly explained that Vance sometimes spoiled his suits during his lab work and the items were approved.

Vance wasn't given long to dwell on his dwindling salary or the attempts on his life. By the end of May, he was sent up to the small southern Interior town of Merritt, BC, where he would work on one of the worst criminal cases in the province's history.

The wrecked Model B Ford is shown in the foreground just below the Merritt-Spence's Bridge Road, taken from the direction of Merritt in May 1934. *Courtesy of the Vance family*

SWEAT

On Wednesday, May 23, 1934, Constable Perry Carr of the Provincial Police in Merritt received a call that there had been a stabbing at the Canford Indian Reserve. Carr called the local GP, and he and Dr John Gillis drove out to the reserve, about twelve miles (twenty km) west of Merritt where the Nooaitch band ranched and farmed.

When they arrived at the reserve, they found that Mary Ann George had been stabbed repeatedly by her husband Eneas George, and had lost a lot of blood. Eneas had taken off, but Carr's immediate concern was to get the woman to Merritt's hospital. He told the family he'd be back later that night to talk to Eneas. When Carr got back to the station, Alfred Barber, the officer in charge of the Nicola Indian Agency, told him to take Constable Frank Gisbourne with him and arrest Eneas.

Early the next day, several cars as well as the regular morning bus saw a wrecked Model B Ford part of the way down the steep cliff below the Merritt–Spence's Bridge Highway. At least two people investigated, but as they said later, they assumed that the car had run off the road and that the victims had been taken to hospital. Eventually a passerby recognized it as Constable Gisbourne's car and notified police.

Meanwhile, Agent Barber arrived at the police station and was surprised to find a prisoner in the jail who had not been fed. Constable Carr usually had the cell door keys, but he wasn't there. Barber was immediately concerned. He had sent Gisbourne and Carr out to the reserve the night before, and he knew they should have been back hours ago. When he heard about the car crash just east of the reserve,

Crime scene photo of the interior of the blood-stained car taken in May 1934.
Courtesy of the Vance family

he feared that the two constables had been involved in a car accident, so he went to search for the missing officers.

Barber found the abandoned car. It had plunged off the highway and down a trail that led from the reserve. He clambered down the steep incline to the river bank and saw that only a tree had prevented the car from falling into the flood-swollen Nicola River. He noticed that the windshield was splintered, there was a large pool of blood on the running board, and the floor mat was wet. Barber saw a brown shoe that he thought was Gisbourne's. A pair of handcuffs lay in blood in the back seat, and Carr's riding crop lay in the front seat.

Barber noticed two trails leading to the river that looked like they were made by dragging heavy objects through the bush. He followed them to the water's edge. There he found a tattered bit of paper. It was the cover of a copy of the Indian Act, and it had his own handwriting on it. This was the document that he'd given Gisbourne before sending him to the reserve the night before.

Barber scrambled up the bank and drove back to town to report the disappearance of the two officers to police headquarters.

Sergeant William Service and Constable J.A. Carmichael were sent from headquarters in Kamloops to help with the investigation. They drove straight to the car wreck and covered the car with a tarpaulin to protect any fingerprints, blood, and other evidence from being washed away in the rain before they could be properly examined by the forensics team—Inspector Vance of the Vancouver Police Department and Sergeant Rodger Peachey, fingerprint expert with the Provincial Police. Carmichael was left to guard the car.

Vance started with a thorough examination of the car. He cut samples of the stained upholstery and had the mats taken from the floor of the Ford. He collected a tiny piece of fabric from the back seat of the car, and a wisp of blue material he found caught between the right running board and the fender. A dirty scrap of white cloth was wedged in the hinge of the left door, and he extracted another scrap of cloth from the car's floor.

While Vance completed his painstakingly slow examination, Sergeant Peachey took dozens of photographs of the blood-spattered windows and the streaks of blood on the back of the car. Another officer found a bit of cloth caught in a bush a few feet above the water and handed it over to Vance.

Inspector John Shirras was charged with directing the search for the missing policemen.[11] Officers were called in from all over the district. Shirras brought a dozen of them with him and surrounded several of the buildings at what the Nooaitch called Rancherie. The

---

11 In 1942, Shirras was appointed along with industrialist Austin C. Taylor and Frederick Mead, the assistant commissioner of the RCMP, to head up the British Columbia Security Commission, the organization that carried out the uprooting of more than 20,000 Japanese Canadians.

Police officers investigate Rancherie in May 1934. *Courtesy of the Vance family*

reserve included several small shingled houses, an outhouse, and a church surrounded by scattered pine and cottonwood trees. Other officers spread out along the river bank. They could see where the car had left wildly zig-zagged tracks in the dirt before careening over the bank and into the tree. There was blood on the sagebrush and rocky ground where a tree had been cut down. An officer gathered up some glass, which Vance would later be able to fit into the broken window of the crashed car.

Shirras found a piece of human scalp with matted hair still attached lying in a pool of blood near the reserve's gate. As police searched the reserve, they picked up a wooden club that was covered in blood and hair as well as a railway tie covered with spots of what looked like blood. They also found two police-issue flashlights and a stained axe.

Eneas was found in one of the buildings and police arrested him for the stabbing of his wife. His brother Joseph was found at Chief Billy's house. Joseph was taken to the hospital with a serious concussion.

The investigators determined that Constable Percy Carr had been on good terms with the Nooaitch band members. He lived in Merritt

Vance and a detective look for evidence at Rancherie. *Courtesy of the Vance family*

with his wife Margaret and two small girls, and had worked as a police officer for eight years. He refused to carry a gun, believing that it was easier to deal with people when they knew they were not being forced into submission at the point of a revolver. He'd worked with Gisbourne on many cases dealing with Indigenous people in the area. But it was no secret that the officers also had enemies, especially after arrests dealing with illegal homebrew and drunkenness.

Constable Gisbourne, who lived in Canford, was also married and had a son. Before joining the Nicola Indian Agency in 1930, he was district chief of fire protection in Kamloops and had served with the forestry branch for six years. Without naming sources, local newspapers alleged that Gisbourne was known to have been too severe in his dealings with the Nooaitch and there had been threats against his life.

On the following Saturday morning, Attorney General Gordon Sloan announced that the government was offering a $500 reward for recovering the bodies of officers Gisbourne and Carr. Later that day, police got their first break when an Indigenous man from the reserve, known to them as Big Frank, told them that he'd seen a man's body floating in the water near an irrigation ditch on his property about two miles (three km) below the reserve along the Nicola River. When police arrived, they saw that it was Frank Gisbourne's body. His head had been battered almost beyond recognition, and he was missing a shoe.

Police officers and volunteers continued to patrol the river banks, searching shallows and logjams for Carr. They placed nets at strategic points all the way down the river to Spences Bridge in the hope of intercepting his body.

Police took Richardson George, Henry Brown, and Tommy Andrews into the station for questioning. Slowly the story spilled out.

Gisbourne and Carr had arrived on the reserve just after 11:00 p.m. They weren't expecting trouble. Gisbourne parked his car near Chief Billy Ernest's house. He went to arrest Eneas while Constable Carr remained in the Ford. Gisbourne saw the four George brothers—Eneas, Joseph, Richardson, and Alex—coming down the path and went to meet them. Gisbourne shone his flashlight in their faces, and Richardson George called out, "Do you want to fight? Do you want to fight?" Gisbourne replied that he just wanted Eneas.

He asked Eneas to come with him, but Eneas refused. When Gisbourne reached out to grab him, Eneas hit him. As the four men descended upon Gisbourne, the officer pulled out his gun and fired a shot at Joseph George, who was charging him. Joseph fell down, clutching his head. The shot missed, but Richardson didn't know that and thought his brother was dead. Gisbourne, now aware that he was fighting for his life, tried to fire his pistol again, but the gun jammed. He was thrown to the ground, and Richardson hit Gisbourne five times on the head with his own police-issued flashlight. Eneas clung to Gisbourne's feet.

When he heard the gunshot, Constable Carr jumped from the car and ran toward the fight. He was unarmed and told the brothers: "Stop that, stop that. I am not coming here to make trouble, I only want Eneas."

Gisbourne managed to break away and run toward the gate with Richardson and Eneas in pursuit. The brothers caught up with Gisbourne and beat him over the head with a club until they killed him, and then they turned to Carr who had managed to make a run for the police car. The brothers quickly overtook him. Richardson said, "We'll kill that one too, for killing our brother," and they began to beat him.

The brothers loaded Gisbourne's body into the back seat of the police car, then stopped to pick up Carr and put him in the car as well. Alex drove along the trail that led to Merritt, but the car veered into a ditch and crashed into a tree. The brothers couldn't move it.

Richardson's trademark buckskin shirt was covered in blood, his hand was cut, and there was a handcuff hanging from his right wrist that Gisbourne had managed to get on him. He got an axe and a saw from Chief Billy Ernest's house, and also brought back nineteen-year-old Henry Brown to drive the car out of the ditch. Henry tried to back it up, but it wouldn't move. Richardson and Eneas cut down the tree, and Richardson went back to the reserve to get his horse and a rope.

Front view of Rancherie. Chief Billy's house is on the far right, just before the wood-shed. *Courtesy of the Vance family*

A jack pine was the only thing stopping Constable Gisbourne's car from being swept away by the Nicola River in May 1934. *Courtesy of the Vance family*

Finally, they managed to manoeuver the car back up the incline and onto the road. At this point, Carr started to moan. Richardson got out of the car, found a rock, and bashed his head in. He searched the dead officer's uniform until he found the keys to unlock the handcuffs.

Henry Brown drove the car down the trail to the main highway, and the men pushed it over the bank with the police officers still inside. The car struck a boulder near the edge of the road, and instead of careening down the bank into the river as the George brothers intended, it lodged against a Jack pine. Richardson went down the bank to the car, and with Brown's help dragged out the bodies and threw them into the swiftly flowing Nicola River. After that, they took everything back to the chief's house. Richardson gave ten dollars to Henry Brown and told him not to say anything to anyone about what he had seen.

Twenty-one-year-old Alex George, the youngest of the four brothers, wasn't on the reserve and couldn't be found. He stayed on the run for four days before turning himself into police. On Tuesday, May 29, he took Inspector Shirras up to the hill just south of the reserve and showed him where they had hidden a pair of trousers, a pair of overalls,

Police search Rancherie in May 1934. *Courtesy of the Vance family*

Richardson's buckskin shirt, and the red shirt he had worn the night of the murder. Shirras also found a notebook with Gisbourne's name in it, a key ring, and a police baton. Everything was sent to Vance.

Alex, Eneas, and Richardson George were charged with murder. Joseph's case was more complex. He was still deaf, likely from the gunshot blast that went off near his ear. Joseph couldn't read or write English, and that rendered him "beyond the law of the criminal court." Richardson, Eneas, and Alex George were taken to Oakalla Prison Farm to await trial. Joseph George was taken to St. Paul's Hospital in Vancouver, still unable to hear.

Under Canadian law, "Indians" were considered wards of the Government, and the George brothers were appointed a lawyer for their defence. While the Attorney General himself was acting as prosecutor, the defence team was formidable, comprising veteran criminal defence lawyer Stuart Henderson and Merritt-born Henry Castillou. Castillou, who was one of the first lawyers in BC to work on Aboriginal rights, understood the language of the Nooaitch, and was proud of his rural roots.

DAILY PROVINCE

AY, MAY 28, 1934—28 PAGES   79,190   PRICE THREE CENTS

GHT HOPPERS | Members Greeted | *OXFORD GROUP BACK*
rain Crop Menaced by Post—P. 17 | At Victoria by Premier Pattullo—Many Meetings to Be Held—P. 8

Police Scientists Now Examining Clues from Scene of Nicola Crime

Scene of Attack on Police

Gisborne's Body Is Recovered From River Saturday.

BROTHERS FACE MURDER CHARGE

Inspector Vance and Sergt. Penchey Making Blood Tests.

Police search for evidence at Rancherie. *Daily Province*, May 28, 1934. *Courtesy of the Vance family*

The trial was held at the end of June. Those who could get seats heard first from Big Frank, who had reported seeing a body in the water, several police officers, and a number of members from the Nooaitch Indian Band.

When it was Vance's turn to testify, he started with the evidence that he'd found in the car. He showed the court how a tiny piece of blue cloth had been torn from Eneas George's shirt, while two other scraps of cloth had been ripped from Richardson's shirt. There was human blood on the front of the shirt and on both cuffs. A piece of the left cuff of Richardson's shirt was missing and fitted a scrap found in the police car. Aside from the jig-saw like fit, the dye and texture were exactly the same, Vance said, and there were the same number of threads to the inch. The scrap that the officer had found on the river bank fit into a tear in Richardson's trousers. The evidence clearly put two of the George brothers in the police car.

Vance's tests further showed that the stains on all the exhibits were human blood. That included Richardson's buckskin coat and torn trousers, the blue shirt worn by Eneas George, and Alex George's red shirt, which also had a piece of fabric missing from the right sleeve. The brown shoe found in the car and the one recovered from Gisbourne's body were a pair, Vance said. He knew this conclusively because the construction was identical and the same polish was used on both shoes.

Vance confirmed the presence of human blood on the riding crop, the car mats and upholstery, Constable Carr's key ring (that had been found in Richardson's trouser pocket), and a tree branch picked up from the river bank. He also identified two rocks—one weighing seven pounds (three kg), the other slightly smaller—that were stained with blood, as were handcuffs found on the back seat of the police car. A flashlight that Gisbourne was holding on the night of the murders had blood on the contact point between the glass and the metal, Vance showed. Vance produced blood-saturated soil taken from the reserve and a club covered with blood on all sides. He found blood on a railroad tie, an axe, and a crooked stick taken from the reserve. Vance emphasized that after examining the items for blood stains, he could confirm that it was human blood, but was unable to state if it came from a specific person or people or how long it had been there. "I am not prepared to say that I could tell the blood of an Indian from the blood of a white person," he replied to a question under cross-examination.

In his summation, prosecutor Sloan said: "Gisbourne was brutally [and] mercilessly beaten as he lay helpless on the ground, and he was finished off with a half of a railway tie weighing twenty-five pounds [eleven kg]. It was a blow from this brutal instrument, I submit, that smashed his skull and drove the nineteen pieces of bone into the brain."

The jury took two hours to return a verdict of guilty for three of the George brothers. Justice Dennis Murphy issued the death sentence. The fourth brother, Joseph George, was found not guilty, as he'd been knocked unconscious before the murders took place.

But while Vance's evidence placed the George brothers at the scene of the murder, and the testimony from members of the Nooaitch band established their guilt, it was Vance's findings from his examination of

This jury found Richardson, Eneas, and Alex George guilty of murder in 1935. Photo taken on the roof of the courthouse, with the second Hotel Vancouver in the background. *Vancouver Archives CVA 99-4808*

Constable Gisbourne's gun that gave the defence grounds for appeal. Vance testified that he had examined the automatic pistol carried by Gisbourne and established that the single shot fired came from that gun. He said that the shot was one of a clip of six and that the gun had jammed after the first shell refused to eject from the breech. Defence lawyers Henderson and Castillou appealed on the grounds that the George brothers had killed the policemen in self-defence. They proposed that Gisbourne had shot at the brothers, who believed he had killed their brother. The Georges had good reason to think that, once he fixed the jammed automatic, Gisbourne would shoot all of them. In self-defence, therefore, they seized the weapon and attacked Gisbourne. The actions of the police, said Henderson, were "illegal and unreasonable ... Had Gisbourne's gun not jammed, in all likelihood, it is he who would have been on trial charged with the murder of four Indians."

Constable Percy Carr's body wasn't recovered until after the trial, and the legal battle dragged on. Despite the appeal, which resulted in a new seventeen-day trial and a recommendation for mercy from the jury, Richardson and Eneas George went to the gallows on November 6, 1936. Alex George was sentenced to life in prison. Joseph lived the rest of his life at the Coldwater Indian Reserve and died at the age of ninety-one in 1987.

If Vance had hoped to take time off with his family that summer, he would be sadly disappointed. After testifying at the trial of the George brothers, he arrived back in Vancouver to find several cases vying for his attention.

The attempted assassinations on Vance's life made front-page headlines. *Daily Province*, October 6, 1934. *Courtesy of the Vance family*

FEAR

On July 11, 1934, Nanaimo, BC, Crown Prosecutor Arthur Leighton wrote to Inspector Vance requesting his assistance. "There have been several safes blown in Nanaimo in the last year or so and we wonder if it could be possible for you by examination of the old safes or dials to connect any of the tools which have been seized with these operations." Leighton also sent to Vance envelopes containing dust and pieces of fabric that were found at the burglaries as well as clothing they had retrieved from the suspect's house. George Hannay was charged with possession of dynamite and burglary tools including a stolen stone mason's hammer.

Vance wrote back to Leighton telling him he'd be pleased to assist. He was testifying at an inquest in Kamloops on July 16, and giving evidence for two separate criminal cases on July 17 and 18. They arranged to meet in Nanaimo, on Vancouver Island, on July 19.

Hannay, the suspected safecracker, was a former Provincial Police officer who'd had a distinguished career acting directly under the chief constable of Nanaimo. In 1913, he left his wife and their two children and took off to California with twenty-three-year-old Mary Catherine, the Catholic daughter of a local barber. While there, he served a fifteen-month jail sentence for forgery and was then deported back to Canada where he faced another three years in jail for misappropriating government funds prior to his departure for the US. Once he served his time, Hannay stayed in Nanaimo and went into safecracking. It wasn't a great career choice because he wasn't very good at it; George spent most of the 1920s in jail for a variety of offences that included breaking into a Port Alberni drugstore.

Hannay, now fifty-three years old, was suspected of blowing a safe at Buckerfield's warehouse the previous December and a robbery at the Nanaimo and District Farmer's Co-operative Association in April 1934. He was also a person of interest in the most recent robbery at Pearson's Sales, where the safe was cracked with nitroglycerin, lard, and a double six-foot (two-metre) length of bell wire attached to a percussion cap. The explosion had blown the safe door through two glass partitions and it landed forty feet (12 metres) away. The thieves had made off with just eleven dollars. While they had worn gloves and not left fingerprints, Hannay had been seen casing the warehouse with his associate William Jones a few days before the robbery. Shoe imprints found at the crime scene were the same as those found at the other two robberies. When police searched Hannay's house they found 321 sticks of sixty-percent dynamite, a Listerine bottle of nitroglycerin, sixty detonators, some with wires attached, as well as a number of tools including an auger. Hannay explained that all the materials were used in his mining operations.

The *Nanaimo Free Press* announced that the Crown had retained Vance's services to testify against George Hannay. After hearing Vance's scientific evidence at the preliminary hearing, Hannay, who was representing himself, reserved his defence and was taken to Oakalla to await his trial the following October.

By Friday, October 5, 1934, there hadn't been an attack on Vance's life for several months, so when the brakes failed on his car at Oak Street and 25th Avenue, which made him almost crash into a streetcar, he chalked it up to mechanical problems. He didn't tell police right away but described the near miss in his notes that night: "I put my foot lightly on the brakes, it was just the slightest touch. Immediately the car skidded sideways and swerved this way and that, and finally swung around in a complete turn. It was almost as if I had jammed on the brakes on a wet pavement."

A little before 9:00 the next morning, Vance went to the garage at the back of his house, got into his car, and tried to start it. The engine refused to turn over. Vance found that it would only run for a second after he took his foot off the starter. He was startled when his eldest son Jack came running from the house and yelled, "Dad, there's something under the car." Vance leaped out and saw that there was a lighted fuse. He tore it off and put out the flame. The fuse was attached to a small package of explosives hidden under the gas tank. Someone had tampered with the car's engine so that the fuse, which was stuffed up the exhaust pipe, would light when the car was started. Vance tossed the package and fuse into his back yard and called police. He and the detectives then took the package to a nearby vacant lot, relit the fuse, and ran for cover. They watched as the flame reached the package and then exploded.

Detectives found that Vance's garage had been broken into the night before and the bomb attached to the car's undercarriage.

The seventh attempt on Vance's life occurred only a couple of days later, and also took place at his home. On October 8, the Monday of the Thanksgiving weekend, Vance was working at the lab and came home for an early dinner before heading out again to catch the steamer to Nanaimo where he was scheduled to give evidence at George Hannay's trial.

When Vance got out of his car, he noticed that a window in his garage—the same one used for the break-in a few days before—had been left open. As Vance stretched out his right hand to close the window, a man who had been crouched below waiting for him jumped up and hurled a jar of acid at him. Instinctively, Vance threw up his hands to

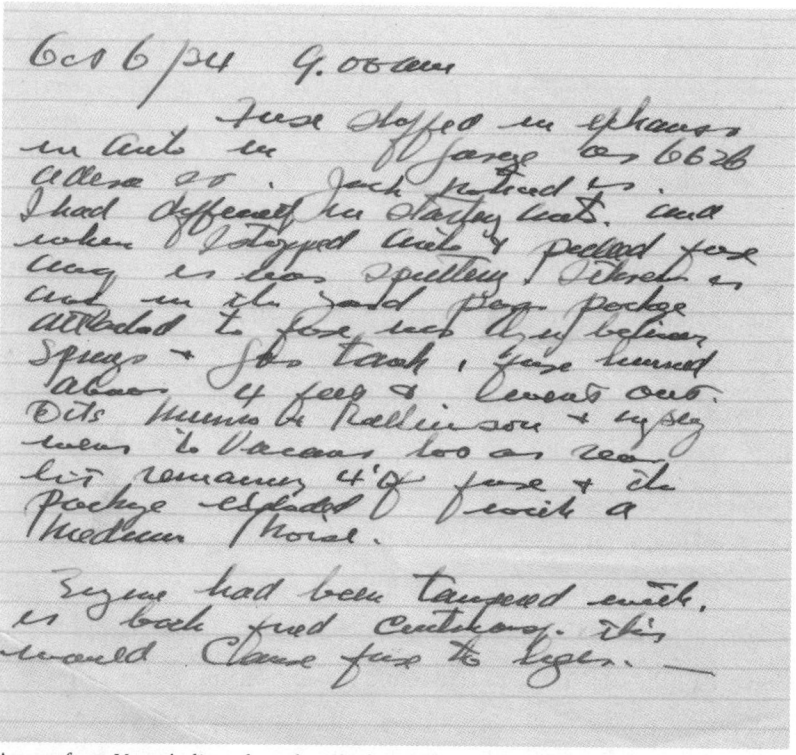

A page from Vance's diary describes the bomb that was put in his car. *Courtesy of the Vance family*

protect his face just before he felt the liquid splash his hands and clothing.

His screams brought Ethel Vance running. She called for their son Tom to phone police and helped her husband back into the house where she applied water and baking soda to the burns. A few drops of acid penetrated through his fingers and burned his right eyebrow, but the worst burns were on his legs. The acid had eaten through his trousers, which now hung off him in shreds. The burns on his left knee and both hands and legs felt like they were on fire.

Sergeant Alex McAfee answered the police call and was at the Vance house within minutes. Seeing the seriousness of Vance's injuries, McAfee put Vance in the police car and rushed him to Vancouver General Hospital. Vance was treated in emergency and later moved to

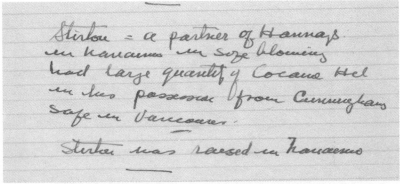

Vance connects Stirton to George Hannay in this diary entry of October 16, 1934. *Courtesy of the Vance family*

a private ward where a police officer stood guard all night.

Vance's two sons Jack and Tom and a neighbour had already started to search the bush behind the house, and police scoured the grounds and surrounding neighbourhood. The attacker had fled through an overgrown lot at the back of the house and into a lane that ran between Adera and Granville Streets.

Jack told police that he had been in the garage on the afternoon of the acid attack, and at that time the window was properly closed. Police found the jar that had contained the sulphuric acid under the window of the garage. They also found a crudely printed note on a wrinkled piece of paper pinned to the wall of the garage. Vance's name was at the top left-hand corner of the note. Underneath, someone had drawn a skull and scrawled the words: "Blindness." It was signed "Warning of Hannay's pals."

Even after the failed bomb attempt two days earlier, police guards had not resumed their duties at the house, and Vance was not given a bodyguard or driver. In fact, it had been months since Vance had any kind of police protection at all.

Later that night, Chief Cameron, Deputy Chief John Murdoch, and Chief Inspector A.G. McNeil crowded into Vance's hospital room to

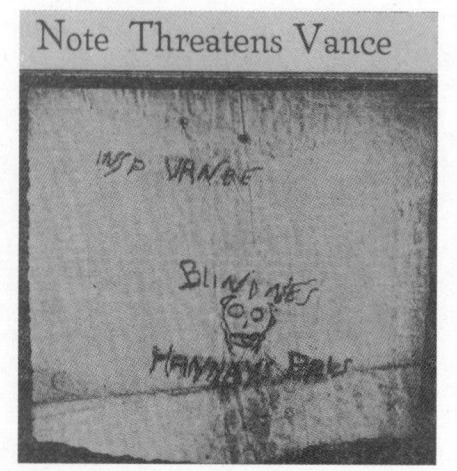

Note Threatens Vance

A note is found pinned to a wall in Vance's garage after he is attacked with acid. *Daily Province,* October 10, 1934. *Courtesy of the Vance family*

get a description of his attacker. Vance told them that he was a thin-faced man with a long nose, dark hair, about forty-five years old, and around five-foot-eleven (180 cm).

The latest attack made the front page of every daily in Vancouver, Victoria, and Nanaimo, and reporters camped outside the hospital. Vance, still swathed in bandages, coached police officers from his hospital bed on how to collect and preserve evidence at his home, including what was left of the suit that he was wearing and which would need to be sent away for testing. He told a reporter from the *Daily Province*: "I have been threatened in regard to some recent cases and had been careful of taking unnecessary chances. The attempt to bomb me on Saturday put me further on my guard, but I suppose I was careless today owing to the early hour of the attack. One expects an attack of this kind to be made during the hours of darkness."

On October 9, Vance received a letter from his former boss, the ex-Police Chief William Bingham. "How glad am I to note that you have again, unaided, escaped your enemies. Press comments are keeping you in the glare of the spotlight and is one of the reasons for repeated attempts to harm you. You are fearlessly performing your duties, hence the attempts," wrote Bingham. "That I would love to help you in this extremity is beyond question, but any action of mine will be misinterpreted. Insist upon proper protection—you are too valuable as both expert and friend to lose in this way."

DAILY PROVINCE

)AY, OCTOBER 6, 1934 —54 PAGES   CIRCULATION YESTERDAY. 78,706   PRICE TEN CENTS

LS TO COWS | Sermons In Gaelic *DEDICATE CHURCH*
s to B. C. Dairy Farm — Page 22 | and In English to Inaugurate Life of Kirk In Mt. Pleasant—Page 28

Vance Escapes Death Plot Again as His Son Finds Bomb Under Car

Two days after the attack, Vance was still on the front page of the three Vancouver newspapers. *Daily Province*, October 6, 1934. *Courtesy of the Vance family*

Newspapers reported that Chief Inspector McNeill had made up a list of men sent to prison at least in part because of Vance's testimony in court. They had all been checked and released, he said. "Some of the ex-cons admitted that they resented Vance at the time of their convictions," wrote a reporter. "'It is just like losing in a card game,'" said one. "'The police held better cards than I did, and I could not make a bluff stand up. The game was square. No one kicks at losing in a square game.'"

Two days after the attack, Vance was still on the front page of the three Vancouver newspapers. The *Daily Province* ran the headline: "Vance to Have Twenty-Four-Hour-a-Day Armed Guard, City to Take No Chance with Life of Criminologist," and reported that from now on, Vance would use only protected police cars. Inspector Rod McLeod was put in charge of investigating his case.

Chief Cameron told the reporter: "Mr Vance was told repeatedly not to use his own car, and to take full advantage of the protection we gave him. He did not seem to want it and continued to use his own automobile. As late as Saturday when I had intended to leave town for a day, I called him and told him to be careful and to take no chances. From now on, it will be not what Mr Vance wants, but what I want." The chief said an armed guard would be placed at the Vance home twenty-four hours a day in three eight-hour shifts. Vance would be under police protection everywhere he went.

But while to the public Chief Cameron appeared to be taking a tough stance, Vance's notebook tells a different story. Stories circulated that some detectives were jealous of the attention that Vance received from his work and because of his newspaper headlines. Vance began to believe that the attacks on his life might be an inside job, maybe even coming from the chief himself.

While Vance was recuperating, George Stirton, the man thought to be behind the earlier attempt on his life, sent word from prison that he felt that he had received a fair deal at his trial and that Vance's deductions were correct. Stirton, Vance knew, was originally from Nanaimo, and an old pal of Hannay's.

George Hannay's trial was moved to a later date to give Vance time to recover. At home, Vance discovered that the papers and notes that he had placed in the door pocket of his car in preparation for the trip to Nanaimo had been stolen. Vance left for Nanaimo under the guard of Inspector McLeod and Sergeant R. Owens of the Provincial Police.

In his notebook, Vance wrote that when they boarded the *Princess Elaine* for Nanaimo, he was asked to put his black bag with the ointment needed to treat his burns in the chief steward's room. Later that night, he and Corporal Paul Corrigan were going over some notes for the case in Vance's room at the Malaspina Hotel. "As my legs pained, I loosened the bandages and applied new ointment from the can that I had received from the hospital in Vancouver to my legs and left hand. Within a short time both legs started to burn. My legs, head, and arm became burning and inflamed and the pain became unbearable." Corrigan called in Inspector McLeod, who told him the bandages were probably too tight, and Vance told Corrigan to go to bed, he would see a doctor in the morning.

"I walked the floor until about 4:00 a.m. The wounds were burning at a terrific rate," Vance wrote. By the next morning, Vance's wounds were blistered, and Corrigan took him to the hospital in Nanaimo. While Vance believed the ointment had been tampered with on the boat, he was determined to continue on as the principal Crown witness in the trial against Hannay that afternoon.

As expected, the courtroom was packed, and those who couldn't get seats were jammed in the corridors to try to hear Vance's testimony. Vance slowly and methodically took the jury through his evidence. He showed them that material taken from the cuffs of Hannay's trousers contained mica, red brick, fire brick, particles of wood, silica sand, oxidized metal, and specks of rust. These materials, he said, exactly matched the substances taken from a pigeonhole in the safe. Vance demonstrated how a splinter of wood found in Hannay's coat pocket fit into a floorboard taken from the scene of one of the robberies. He verified that the shreds of cloth found on the premises not only contained the same dye, the same dust, and the same pattern of threads as those in the suit taken from Hannay's home, but also fit exactly into the tears in the material.

Hannay's defence lawyer, Joseph Edward Bird,[12] stayed at the same hotel where Vance was. Vance wrote: "A continual stream of more or less disreputables were coming and going to Bird's room. On Wednesday night, Bird was heard to tell Tom Moore [the main witness for the defence] that Hannay was sunk. That the prosecution evidence was too strong. Moore and the others must get something, trump up something at any cost otherwise Hannay was lost."

---

12   In 1914, Bird represented the passengers from India on board the *Komagata Maru*. He fought against their deportation, and although unsuccessful, challenged Canada's highly restrictive immigration laws. He was an advocate for equality and sought to reform the race-based exclusion laws in Canada.

The next morning, the crowd got some unexpected drama when Bird said that the Crown's main evidence, produced by Corporal Corrigan and analysed by Vance, was "all made up" and that the jury "had a lot of false evidence crammed down their throats."

"I was the first witness at 10:00 a.m., and I was immediately subject to cross-examination by Bird for an hour and three-quarters," wrote Vance. "He was exceedingly dirty and showed by his cross-examination that he had knowledge of the papers that were stolen from my car."

After deliberating for less than two hours, the jury announced they could not agree. Eleven voted for conviction, and one, whom Vance noted was a friend of Hannay's, voted for acquittal. "The eleven could not move this man who appeared to be the foreman of the jury," wrote Vance. "I protested to Mr Leighton [the prosecutor] the fact that Hannay would be free on a $2,000 bail until the spring assize, and I did not like the prospect of his being free to direct more assaults against me. He stated that nothing could be done in the matter and it would have to take its course."

After the trial, Vance noted in his journal that Hannay approached him. "He said that I must not blame him for the acid-throwing episode as he would not do such a thing, but that he was not responsible for the actions of his friends."

WATSON

Outside the police station and in the newspapers, Police Chief Cameron stood solidly behind Vance. He praised his achievements, supported his inventions, and appeared to put the full force of the Vancouver Police Department behind the Vance family's safety. But Vance's personal notebook tells a different story. He still suspected that the chief was behind the attacks on his life—or at the very least knew who was. But by the fall of 1934, Cameron's own position looked shaky.

It looked as though Cameron's biggest supporter, Mayor L.D. Taylor, would lose the upcoming election to his archrival, a lawyer named Gerry McGeer. McGeer promised to clean up corruption at City Hall and inside the VPD, and his slogan "Are you for me or the underworld?" appealed to civilians fed up with the prostitution, gambling, bootlegging, and drugs that troubled the city. L.D. had lost control, and Cameron's days were also numbered.

Vance's notebook tells the story of an out-of-control, alcoholic chief of police who was often seen drinking in his office and inebriated at restaurants and seedy hotels in the downtown area. Cameron, along with other senior officials and at least two magistrates, seemed to enjoy flaunting his power at the expense of honest cops.

And Vance was scrupulously honest. When the Attorney General sent him a cheque over and above his usual reimbursement of expenses, he sent the money back. "I wish to thank you most sincerely for your kindly thought in sending the cheque for $250.00," Vance wrote. "Unfortunately, I am not permitted to accept any monies for my services, not even as a gift or token of appreciation."

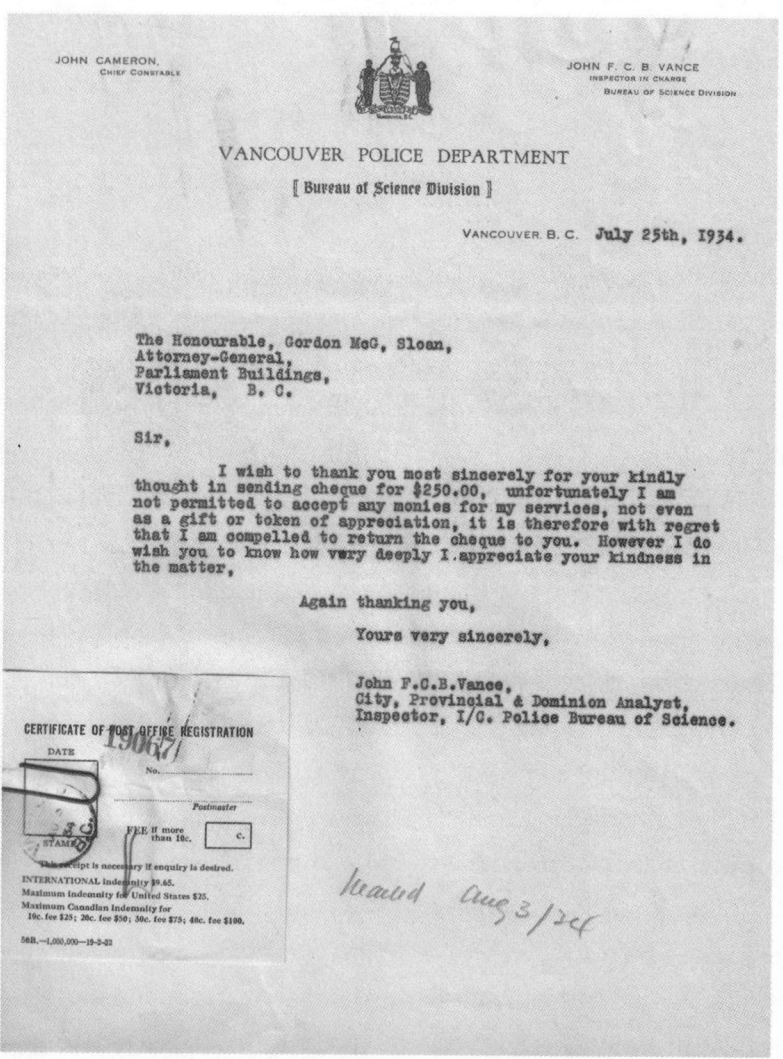

JOHN CAMERON,
CHIEF CONSTABLE

JOHN F. C. B. VANCE
INSPECTOR IN CHARGE
BUREAU OF SCIENCE DIVISION

VANCOUVER POLICE DEPARTMENT

[Bureau of Science Division]

VANCOUVER. B. C. **July 25th, 1934.**

The Honourable, Gordon McG. Sloan,
Attorney-General,
Parliament Buildings,
Victoria, B. C.

Sir,

I wish to thank you most sincerely for your kindly
thought in sending cheque for $250.00, unfortunately I am
not permitted to accept any monies for my services, not even
as a gift or token of appreciation, it is therefore with regret
that I am compelled to return the cheque to you. However I do
wish you to know how very deeply I appreciate your kindness in
the matter.

Again thanking you,

Yours very sincerely,

John F.C.B.Vance,
City, Provincial & Dominion Analyst,
Inspector, I/C. Police Bureau of Science.

CERTIFICATE OF POST OFFICE REGISTRATION
DATE
No.

Postmaster
FEE if more
than 10c.   c.
STAMP
This receipt is necessary if enquiry is desired.
INTERNATIONAL indemnity $9.65.
Maximum indemnity for United States $25.
Maximum Canadian indemnity for
10c. fee $25; 20c. fee $50; 30c. fee $75; 40c. fee $100.
56B.—1,000,000—19-3-32

Vance returns the $250 he received from the Attorney General for his work in the
murder of two constables in Merritt earlier in the year. *Courtesy of the Vance family*

Wild rumours circulated at police headquarters that Vance talked
with McGeer and that he might even replace Cameron as the chief of
police. Vance confronted the chief. "I told him that things seemed at
variance between us and could use straightening out," Vance wrote in
his notebook. "He said: 'What do you mean? I do not know what you

A page from Vance's diary describes a meeting with Chief Cameron and Magistrate McKay about rumours circulating around Vance. *Courtesy of the Vance family*

are talking about, ... He said 'Why don't you come to me when you hear these things?' I said 'I am here now.'"

Cameron did nothing to hide the fact that he was friends with brothel operators like Joe Celona and Clarence Bancroft. He was a regular at Celona's Maple Hotel, which had illegal gambling downstairs and a brothel upstairs. Celona, who'd been shot by his wife Josie the previous December (see Chapter 6), was often seen at the police station delivering booze to the chief. Celona was a frequent guest at Cameron's swanky Shaughnessy home as well as at his ranch at Port Haney. At one point, Cameron and Celona were seen cruising around Howe Sound in a police boat, sipping cocktails while being entertained by a piper from the police band brought along for the occasion.

By the end of October, the round-the-clock police guard had dropped to the hours of 4:00 p.m. to midnight, and Vance was back to driving himself to and from work. On October 31, Vance wrote: "Halloween night, no guard all day and all night. PC Morphett did not show up. No relief came, no police guard at all."

An entry in his notebook dated November 3, 1934 said that Dennis Clark, a reporter with the *News Herald*, had dropped by to see Vance in his lab. "Clark said that Inspector McLeod [the same officer in charge of the investigation into Vance's assaults] is a known crook and should have been in the pen long ago," wrote Vance. "He said that the story downstairs is that Vance was warned not to use his own car, but when he insists on doing so, the fault is entirely his."

Fortunately, the Sherlock Holmes of Canada had a secret weapon. He had his very own Watson. And, if Vance saw any irony in this, it didn't show up in his notes.

George Watson, a former prison guard, was now a janitor for the Vancouver Police Department, and as such had a key to every office in the building, including the chief's. As janitor, he had a certain cloak of invisibility, and he was privy to the conversations of senior police officers, magistrates, and city officials. He passed much of this information along to Vance.

Watson told Vance that he had seen a two-page handwritten letter on the chief's desk from Detective Duggan that accused Vance of tampering with a records book from a drug case in 1926 and then conspiring with Gerry (Gerald Grattan) McGeer to give false evidence in court. Duggan said in his letter to the chief that he was prepared to give this evidence under oath. McGeer had taken a prominent role in the Lennie Commission, an inquiry into police corruption in 1928, which had cost Chief Henry Long his job and Mayor L.D. Taylor the next election. "Watson said if it was known he read these letters and

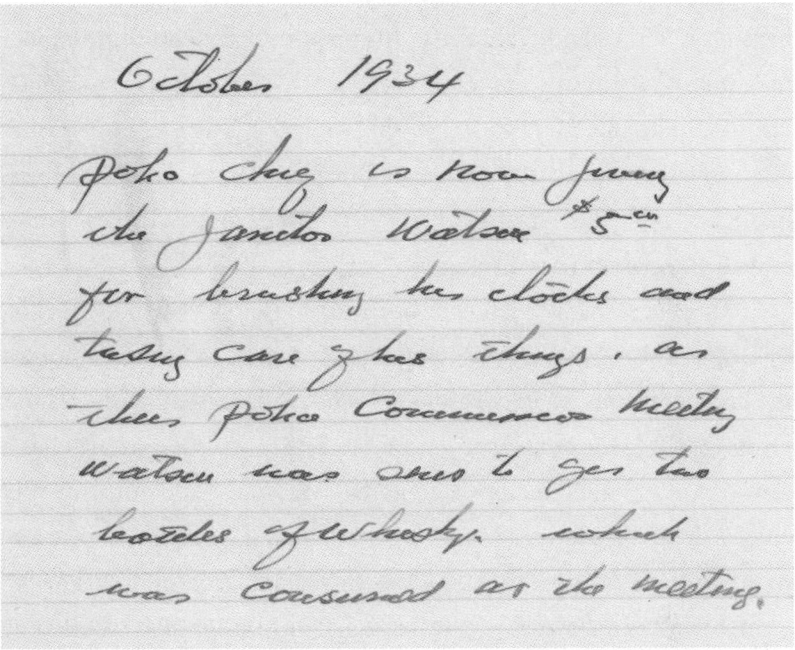
October 1934

Police chief is now giving the janitor Watson $5.00 for brushing his clothes and taking care of his things. at these police commission meeting Watson was sent to get two bottles of whisky. which was consumed at the meeting.

Vance's diary entry of October 1934 after a meeting with janitor George Watson.
Courtesy of the Vance family

divulged their contents, it would cost him his job," Vance wrote. "But he said he would sooner have his wife and children starve than hear such an injustice done Vance."

The following day, Watson stole the incriminating letter from the chief's office and gave it to Vance to photograph. "He gave it to me for the day and asked that I give it back to him at 8:10 a.m. on Monday. He said that Duggan was a dirty rat. He mentioned about drug addicts always hanging around the Broadway Café, that the whole of the Broadway Café is a house of prostitution, and the chief of police is always there."

Vance's notes say that he was told by a trusted source that Duggan's letter was to be used by Mayor Taylor to discredit McGeer in the election, but in the end, even the mayor thought it "too dirty" to use. Watson told Vance that Police Chief Cameron would give him five dollars to brush his clothes and take care of his things. At police commissioner meetings, Watson was sent out to get the whiskey that was consumed on the public tab. He told Vance that after the police commissioner meetings there were always empty bottles lying around Cameron's office, and at the last meeting, there were three empty whiskey bottles and all the glasses were broken.

"The office door was left wide open and the letter written to the chief by Duggan about myself was lying on top of the chief's desk amongst the broken glasses, so it had apparently been discussed," wrote Vance. He notes that Duggan was promoted to sergeant at that meeting as a reward for writing the fabricated letter. "Watson said that the deputy chief is drinking pretty hard and is always in Magistrate McKay's office in the station," wrote Vance. "McKay is with the graft up to his neck."

A couple of days later, Watson brought Vance an envelope containing strands of a carpet confiscated in a recent police raid; the carpet was valued at $1,200. "The chief would not allow this rug to go into the property clerk to be entered in the official way," wrote Vance. "He had it stowed in another room then brought back to his office. Watson suspects the chief wants to steal it and either sell it or take it home. It's a beautiful rug and it has been kept out of sight."

On November 20, the guards disappeared from Vance's house altogether.

Meanwhile, McGeer was threatening an all-out war on crime. He vowed that he would get rid of slot machines and do away with all gambling, book-making, white slavery, and corruption in the police force. In one campaign speech he told his captive audience: "I'm going to clean up on the criminals. Look at them—friends of the mayor—friends of the chief of police; why, Chief Cameron even takes that notoriously evil white-slaver Joe Celona out for cruises in the police boat! And the gamblers, they're operating wide open. You can see for yourself that they must be paying lots of money to policemen to look the other way. Well, you can tell those thugs that Gerry is coming, and if they know what's good for them, they will get out of town."

The voters lapped up McGeer's rhetoric, and he won the election, taking close to eighty percent of the popular vote. On December 31, after a brief demotion to chief detective inspector, Cameron resigned. He wasn't the only casualty. McGeer launched an investigation into the two other members of the police commission, magistrates J.A. Findlay and W.M. McKay. Deputy Chief John Murdoch lasted three days as acting chief constable and was suspended along with sixteen other officers, including the newly minted Sergeant Harry Duggan.

Cameron was replaced by Colonel William Foster, a former military man and politician dedicated to stamping out the Communist threat to Vancouver. Foster brought in Major T.G. McLelan as his legal advisor. McLelan reported that organized crime had thrived under police protection, that well-known criminals operated with the knowledge of ex-Chief John Cameron, and as a result, violent crime was rampant.

Joe Celona, who was already facing a charge of living off the avails of prostitution, was charged along with Cameron with conspiring to create public mischief. Cameron beat the charge, but Celona was hauled off to court for another sensational trial. He was convicted of procuring two servant girls aged sixteen and twenty-one to work at his brothel on the top floor of the Maple Hotel. This time, even his lawyer, Stuart Henderson, couldn't get him off. Celona was sentenced to eleven years in jail.

The evidence presented—of bribe-taking and general corruption—was so damning that the resulting report recommended dismissals of twelve of the seventeen suspended officers and a demotion for another. After a lengthy fight in the courtroom and through the media, Angelo Branca, the scrappy East End lawyer, had all seventeen officers reinstated.

As for Vance, he continued his work under the new regimen without the constant fear of personal attack. With the exception of a feature in the *National Home Monthly* in the fall of 1935 and his appearance as a (probably reluctant) candidate for the Canadian Hall of Fame in *Liberty Magazine*'s May issue of that year, Vance disappeared from the front pages and the headlines of BC's newspapers. This was almost certainly a way to keep him safe.

The use of forensics to solve crimes through science was now becoming more mainstream. In the United States, for instance, the Federal Bureau of Intelligence's crime laboratory had been operating since 1932 with state-of-the-art equipment, including an ultraviolet light machine, a microscope, a moulage kit (for making molds of shoeprints, tire tracks, or other impressions made at a crime scene), a wiretapping kit, photographic supplies, chemicals, and a drawing board.

VICTORIA'S GHOST

Following a request by Police Chief Foster in early 1937, Vance submitted a report that detailed the assistance his Bureau of Science had given to other police organizations. Between January 1934 and September 1936, he wrote, there were forty-nine cases from outside of Vancouver, each taking an average of one to three days' work. As was customary, Vance noted, no charge was made for these services. The cases covered every municipality in the Lower Mainland as well as several communities on Vancouver Island and in the Fraser Valley. The crimes ranged from liquor law violations to breaking and entering, the death of a cow in New Westminster, the death of an inmate in Oakalla Prison Farm, arson, and murder. One of those cases was in Oak Bay, a suburb of Victoria on Vancouver Island.

On Saturday, September 26, 1936, readers of the *Daily Colonist* learned that Victor Gravlin, a former sports reporter at the newspaper, and his estranged wife Doris had been missing for four days. Police, the article said, would be conducting a search in the Oak Bay area for the Gravlins after other means of investigation had failed to turn up any trace of the missing couple.

Victor and Doris married in 1929, had a son named Robin, and separated less than six years later. Doris and her son Robin now lived with her parents. On the night she disappeared, Doris had been at work as a home care nurse to an elderly woman who lived in an apartment on Beach Drive. Doris had told her employer that she was going out for a walk and would be back in a little while. She didn't return.

Both Doris's and Victor's parents reported them missing the next

Photo of Oak Bay Beach Hotel in 1929. *Oak Bay Archives # 2002-001-008*

day. Victor's mother said she'd last seen her son around 8:30 p.m. when she went next door; he wasn't at home when she returned later. She told police that her son had been released from hospital about two weeks before and was convalescing at the time of his disappearance. Victor was well-known in Victoria, and people who knew him said he couldn't handle his whiskey and was a nasty drunk. At the end of 1934, when Victor left the *Daily Colonist* after ten years on the sports desk, Doris took Robin and moved back in with her mother Charlotte and stepfather Robert Thomson on Dallas Road. Charlotte ran a nursing home called Sunhill Sanitorium out of a house in Royal Oak, and Doris often worked and stayed there.

Victor's nephew, George Hetherington, told police that when his uncle was in the hospital he had asked him to deliver letters to Doris at the Sunhill Sanitorium. Once, he said, he had helped Victor take the streetcar to visit his wife in Oak Bay. Hetherington said he didn't know what was in the notes and hadn't heard their conversations, but assumed that Victor was working on a reconciliation with his wife.

Five days after their disappearance, the *Colonist* ran headshots of the couple in the Sunday paper. Thirty-six-year-old Victor was described as five-foot-eleven (180 cm) with a medium build, thin features, and "of nervous temperament." Doris, aged thirty, was five-foot-six (168 cm) with auburn hair and large brown eyes. When last seen, she was wearing a green dress, blue coat with silver buttons, and a grey hat.

When they were together, Victor and Doris often spent their Sundays walking across the golf course to the Oak Bay Beach Hotel. After the article in the *Colonist*, police were told of a possible sighting of the couple near the golf course on the same night as their disappearance. A woman who lived nearby said she'd heard a scream some time after 9:00 that night from the direction of the golf course.

Victoria police searched the bush and shoreline in the area with a bloodhound and a tracker. Police Chief John Syme said that they'd found "indications of a violent struggle" in a clump of broom just off Beach Drive. The soil was disturbed, the grass flattened, there were deep marks in the ground, and there was a lot of blood, he said. At 3:40 that afternoon, John Johnson, a caddy at the Victoria Golf Club, was searching along the waterfront at the edge of the golf course for a lost ball when he caught a glimpse of what look like a pink sweater tucked between some logs. As he went to pick up the sweater, he realized he was looking at the body of a woman. He told some boys who were nearby to run to the clubhouse and call police.

Chief Syme and Constable Walter Douglas met Johnson at a rocky, isolated part of the beach that was covered in driftwood, long grass, shrubs, and wild roses. They found Doris lying in a shallow sand trap at the base of a nine-foot (three-metre) high embankment. She was lying on her back, well-hidden by the long grass. Syme counted five pieces of driftwood laid across the body, over the pink sweater; a smaller piece of wood had been laid across her head, and more branches and seaweed placed on top.

Photo of the area around the Victoria Golf Course and Beach Drive, c.1910. *Oak Bay Archives # 2013-017-022*

Inspector Robert Owens of the Provincial Police and coroner Dr Harold McNiven arrived and saw that her dress was badly matted with blood and had been pulled up underneath her body as though she had been dragged some distance by the legs. She wasn't wearing any shoes, and her stockings had holes in the knees. Her body was badly bruised, she'd been beaten about the head, and there were blood stains around her neck and chest. A large red mark ran across her neck where she had been strangled.

"The body was well covered," said Syme. "I had searched that particular spot with a flashlight two nights previously and saw nothing." The bloodhound that had been brought to the area was "very much disturbed," and led them from that point down a trail to the beach—a distance of 160 yards (146 metres).

The five-man Oak Bay Police Department was already overloaded with petty crime cases and Chief Syme felt out of his depth dealing with a murder investigation. He contacted the Vancouver Police Department and requested the assistance of their criminologist, Inspector Vance.

Vance flew to Victoria the next day and went straight to the crime scene. He collected hairs from the vegetation and samples of the blood-drenched soil and found pieces of torn fabric. The evidence was carefully marked as were the points where it was found. The torn fabric was later matched to Doris's green dress, her sweater, and her stockings. Back at the lab, he confirmed that the blood stains were human and the blood type matched Doris's. The auburn strands of hair from the site were similar to those taken from Doris's head.

When Vance examined her body at the morgue, he found soil and vegetation under her fingernails where she had dug them into the ground. One piece of driftwood that had covered her body was stained with blood and contained scraps of fabric from her clothes as well as remnants of her hair and flesh. Vance found fragments of rope on the skin of her neck.

The *Vancouver News Herald* reported that Doris's hat and shoes were missing, but a pair of shoes too big for her were found near her body. Victor, who was not a large man, would fit into her shoes, went the story, and it was thought that he escaped to the Lower Mainland dressed as a woman. Except for the article about the couple's disappearance and a story published when Doris's body was found, there was nothing further reported in the *Colonist*, possibly because the newspaper was protecting its former reporter.

Several municipal police forces, the provincial police, and even a Boy Scout troupe were involved in the search for Victor, but it wasn't until a month later that he was found. On October 25, Norman Le Poidevin was rowing along the waterfront when he discovered a body tangled in a bed of kelp in deep water just south of Gonzales Point, west of Victoria. He rowed to shore and notified police.

Chief Syme and Constable L.G. Clayards borrowed his boat and rowed out to the body. Clayards tied a rope around the body and towed it to shore. When they searched the clothing, they found Doris's missing shoes stuffed in the left pocket of his overcoat. Her brown belt and grey hat were in the right pocket of his overcoat, along with a half-empty packet of British Consul cigarettes, a white handkerchief, and a piece of hemp rope. Two days later, the *Colonist* ran a small story.

Vance returned to Victoria to examine the corpse. Even though it had been submerged in water for a long time, he was able to find strands of auburn hair and remnants of Doris's clothing on Victor's overcoat. The hair that Vance had found under Doris's fingernails was similar to that from Victor's head. Vance removed auburn hair from the rope found in Victor's pocket. The back and left shoulder of Victor's coat was drenched in blood—the same type as Doris's. Vance figured that Victor had picked her up, then rested before dragging her the rest of the way to the beach. Victor was heavily dressed for that time of year; underneath his coat, Vance noted, Victor wore a jacket and vest, two sweaters, a shirt, long underwear, and a pair of heavy dark shoes. Because the blood on his coat had dried, Victor could not have entered the water less than twenty-four hours after her death, said Vance.

When they scoured the area around Gonzales Point, Vance collected, from a sharp rock ledge, small pieces of fabric that came from Victor's overcoat, and more scraps of fabric from his trousers, which had torn when he had sat down on the slippery rocks. "It is an ideal place for sitting down. One could have an unobstructed view from where the body was hidden and could see but could not be seen from the back at all," Vance testified at Victor Gravlin's inquest. There was also a sheer drop into the water, where Victor had eventually jumped to his death.

The coroner's jury rendered the verdict that "Victor Gravlin did commit suicide by drowning and was of unsound mind." There was no question in anyone's mind that he had first murdered his wife.

The first recorded sighting of Doris occurred shortly after her death. People talked about seeing a woman either walking along the golf course, crossing Beach Drive near the Oak Bay Beach Hotel, or standing near the water where Victor Gravlin drowned himself. Because most of the sightings occurred at the end of March or in April, she became known as "the April Ghost." At times she was seen standing with her arms outstretched, dressed in a white wedding dress. Those who saw her said she would rush toward them and suddenly shrink into a small pool of light and disappear. Afterward, those who'd seen her reported feeling a change in the atmosphere and a sense of dread.

In 1994, Lon Wood was writing a Halloween story about the April Ghost for the *Times Colonist*, a variation of the paper that Victor Gravlin had worked for some sixty years before. He tracked down Robin Thomson in Staffordshire, England, and asked him about his mother's ghost. Thomson was now in charge of public transport in the Midlands.

Robin Gravlin was adopted by his maternal grandparents, renamed Robin Thomson, and sent to private school on Vancouver Island. After the end of World War II, Robin was sent to England to finish his education at the Royal Military Academy, Sandhurst. Much of his career was spent in the Far East.

Wood was shocked to discover that Thomson had no inkling of his parents' fates. "I was under the false assumption that by then he knew at least rudimentary details of his family history," says Wood. "I was immediately stunned to have been the bearer of this news. He seemed more numb than shocked as he processed the information that his father had committed suicide after murdering his mother." Robin told Wood that he knew nothing about his family history. "This is not old," he said. "It's all news to me." The surprised reporter sent him clippings of the murder-suicide and of the many ghost sightings. When Woods called him again a few weeks later, Thomson told him: "If it's history, then it's there, and it's not going to go away."

Wood says that local legend had it that Doris's spirit was restless and would not leave until her son had been told how her parents met their end. Seven months after the phone call informing him of his unfortunate family history, Thomson, then sixty-five, died of heart failure during a gall bladder operation. Wood had a heart attack later that year, left the *Times Colonist*, and was told he had a one-in-five chance of surviving without a transplant. He continues to survive without a transplant, and to his knowledge, there have been no further sightings of the April Ghost.

A year and a half would pass before Vance was called back to Oak Bay by Chief Syme. Once again, it involved a husband and wife.

THE WIDOW 11

It was almost four in the morning of April 1, 1938, when Annie Patrick woke up to pounding on her front door and a woman's voice calling her name. She found her neighbour standing there in her dressing gown and Cowichan knit socks clutching her little girl, a quilt draped over both of them. Annie invited Vera Colebourne inside and asked her what was wrong. Vera said that they had been robbed and she couldn't wake her husband. While Annie made Vera a cup of tea, Annie's son Bob called the police.

Sergeant Hugh Reston was only minutes away and soon arrived at the Patrick house on Bowker Avenue in Oak Bay. Reston found Vera sitting in a chair with five-year-old Hilda in her arms. "She was greatly agitated and trembling terribly," he later said at the inquest. Vera told him that someone had broken into their house through a window. She'd heard an explosion and seen a flash. Frightened, Vera took Hilda and ran to the neighbour's house. She said that her husband had remained asleep. Vera suggested that the break-in had been made by someone who wanted to steal paint because four cans were missing from their cupboard.

Reston, Bob, and Bob's father Robert Patrick left for the Colebournes' house two doors down. The first thing Reston noticed as he walked along the path to the house was a can of white paint spilled onto the sidewalk. There was another can against the Colebournes' front door, intact and upright. Reston moved the can a few inches so he could open the screen door which he found closed but unlocked. The front door of the house was open with a key in the lock on the outside of the

The "April Fool's Day" shooting received front-page headlines. *Daily Colonist*, April 2, 1938.

door. The house was in darkness so he turned on his flashlight and entered, moving cautiously into the bedroom to the right of the front door. Inside, he found Sidney Colebourne lying dead on the couch with a bullet hole in the middle of his forehead. The pillows, sheets, blankets, and floor were soaked with blood, and blood was still streaming from the man's nose and left ear. His arms were folded across his chest, and the body was still warm to Reston's touch.

Reston asked Robert Patrick to go back to his house and phone Chief John Syme and ask him to summon Dr Lloyd McNiven. While he waited, Reston took a look around the small three-bedroom bungalow. It was still very dark, and there was a touch of frost in the air. The lights wouldn't turn on, and he saw that the main switch on the verandah had been pulled. It looked to him like someone had stood on the paint can to reach the electrical panel. The lights came on when he pushed the switch back down. All the windows were locked except for the one on the west side of the house, which was wide open. A curtain rod lay on the outside of the window sill. The back door was bolted on the inside.

While Reston had initially thought robbery was behind the break-in and murder, the house had not been ransacked, nothing was disarranged, the front door was unlocked, and he noticed that the Colebourne's black and white sheep dog was nowhere to be seen. He knew the dog was left loose at night and was often out chasing cars. In fact, Reston had seen the dog when he'd driven past just a few hours before while on patrol. The dog barked when anyone went near the house.

When Chief Syme arrived, he also noticed the lack of disorder in the house. There was a watch and seventy-five cents in change in the pocket of Sid's blue trousers. As his sergeant had already noted, if a burglar had entered through the open window, the curtain rod on the sill would have been knocked to the floor. A sawhorse outside under the window was clean, with no trace of footprints, grass, or dirt, which would have been left behind if it had been used by a thief breaking into the house.

Syme went to the Patricks' to talk to the widow. Vera told him that they had arrived home at about 10:30 the previous night. Sid had been paid that day and had told her he would give her money to pay the bills. Vera joined Hilda in bed, leaving Sid sitting on the couch counting his money. She remembered her husband putting his wallet on the dresser beside the bed. The next thing she remembered was waking up around midnight when she heard the dog running down the front steps. A few hours later, she woke to an explosion and caught a glimpse of a short man wearing a Mack jacket and holding a flashlight bending over her bed. The front door was open, and the lights wouldn't turn on. Vera said the four tins of white paint that were usually stored in the bedroom closet were missing.

The whole story sounded off to Syme, especially the part about the stolen paint cans. He went back to the Colebourne house to fetch some clothing for Vera, then had her arrange for friends to take care of Hilda. Vera was taken to the police station as a material witness and placed in the charge of the city matron.

On the day of the murder, the newspaper headline that afternoon was "April Fool's Day Slaying." The article reported that Sidney William Colebourne, forty-three years old, had been shot in the head while he

Scene of Early Morning Crime

The Colebournes' home and scene of the shooting at 2230 Bowker Avenue.
Daily Colonist, April 2, 1938.

slept on a couch next to his wife and little daughter.

While Chief Syme thought the robbery theory unlikely, he had the widow give him a description of their valuables and where they were kept. Vera said that Sid kept a rosewood box on the bedroom dresser with his gold watch and diamond tie-pin set, and this was also where she kept a ring with two small diamonds and two gold rings. The chief was unable to find the box with those items, the wallet with the missing cash, or the murder weapon. Either the shooting was done by a burglar or the robbery was a blind to throw police off the track.

Chief Syme tried to piece together the events that led up to the murder. Sid had worked that day as ship's rigger and splicer for the BC Coast Steamship Service. He, Vera, and Hilda usually had dinner on Thursday nights at the house of their friends William and Dorothy Fraser. On the day of the murder, Vera and Hilda were already at the

Frasers' house while William met up with Sid after work. They had a few beers and then stopped on the way home to pick up more beer. After dinner, the two couples played crib, and then William drove the Colebourne family home. Dorothy Fraser told police that earlier in the day Vera had mentioned that she wasn't getting along with her husband, but when they left, they seemed on good terms. Sid, she said, was not drunk, and Vera did not drink, ever.

The Oak Bay police department was still a five-man operation with access to three vehicles. Having worked with Inspector Vance on Doris Gravlin's murder less than two years before, Chief Syme once again requested his help. Vance gave him instructions on how to best preserve the crime scene and asked that the house be under twenty-four-hour-a-day guard until he arrived, that photographs be taken, and the entire house dusted for fingerprints.

The next morning, Vance, Chief Syme, Constable Robert Smith, and Sergeant Albert Bailey from the BC Provincial Police went back to Bowker Avenue to undertake a thorough search of the house. Vance examined the verandah by the front door and noted that the can of paint found underneath the light switch could have been used by a person about five-feet-ten (178 cm) to stand on to pull the switch. He checked the entrance to the house through the open living-room window but could find no visible evidence of someone having entered there recently.

Constable Smith was searching the living room when he noticed that the stove pipe that led from the heater to the chimney was loose. With a rake used to remove soot from the stove, he carefully probed through the soot and ashes until he struck metal. Smith reached in and removed a revolver, which he placed on a piece of paper on the floor. It was a nickel-plated .38 calibre Smith & Wesson. There was a spent cartridge behind the firing pin and a loaded shell in the chamber. He bagged the soot, the ashes, and the gun. Later that morning, Smith found Sid Colebourne's black leather wallet—containing thirty-one dollars, his identity card, and several receipts—inside a baking pan hanging on the kitchen wall.

Meanwhile, Sergeant Bailey found a small cardboard box containing the missing jewellery in the clothes closet, wedged against the door jamb. Bailey dusted the gun, the wallet, and the stove pipe for fingerprints, but found none. However, there was a fingerprint on the can of paint on the verandah, and it was later identified as Vera's.

Vance had all the evidence sent to his lab. He would need to confirm the type of ammunition used to kill Colebourne and the kind of weapon that fired the bullet. He needed to determine if the gun found in the chimney fired the bullet that killed Colebourne, and the distance between the target and the weapon when it was fired.

His next step was to see Dr John Moore, the pathologist, and collect the bullet that had been extracted from Sid Colebourne's brain. The shot had been fired at close range and fractured the base of the skull, which caused a hemorrhage in the brain. The bullet had left ninety tiny but distinct powder marks on Colebourne's head. It was also in two pieces, and when Vance weighed it, he found it to be lighter than the live bullet taken from the cartridge in the revolver. He thought the difference might be because part of the bullet still remained in Colebourne's brain. The two extracted parts were badly battered, but under the microscope, Vance could see that the bullet taken from the brain had a groove with a right-hand twist that matched that of the revolver found in the chimney, which had right-hand rifling.

Vance examined Colebourne's hands for powder marks or lead. There were none, which told him that the wound was not self-inflicted, and from the photographs of the crime scene, he saw that the gun would have been held almost level to Colebourne's head. "When the revolver was handed to me, the spent cartridge was directly under the firing pin and a live cartridge to the right of that. I would say the revolver had recently been fired ... The dust on the revolver is the same type of dust as submitted by Chief Syme taken by him from the chimney in the living-room of the house."

Police told the media that Vance's testimony would have an important bearing on the case. "While Vancouver's ace criminologist, Inspector Vance, began a study of the physical clues at the scene, police investigation of Victoria's April Fool's Day murder turned today to an exhaustive inquiry into the past life of the victim," reported the *Vancouver Sun*.

When Vera and Sid met in January 1931, they were both married to other people. Vera's husband at the time, Clarence Youson, was a twenty-four-year-old labourer whom she had married the previous August. They ran a boarding house on Colville Road. Sid met his first wife, Mary-Jane, shortly after he'd arrived from London, England in 1919. Mary-Jane was a fifty-seven-year-old dressmaker; Sid was twenty-four. Two months after Sid met Vera, Mary-Jane died from a stroke. Vera's husband divorced her shortly afterwards, and she married Sid in May 1931 and moved into the Bowker Avenue house where Sid had lived with Mary-Jane. Their daughter Hilda was born the following year.

Sid started to abuse Vera a month after they were married, she testified at trial. He would slap her face for no apparent reason and once tried to choke her. He frequently used foul language, even in front of little Hilda. Vera had found four love letters in his wallet signed by an Elsa B. Sid took Vera's fur coat and mink stole (both of which had originally belonged to his first wife) and gave them to his mistress. When Vera confronted him, Sid took her to a lawyer and made her sign a document that said: "I do hereby give to Sidney Colebourne one fur coat and one mink neckpiece."

In July 1936, Vera went to see William C. Moresby, K.C., a barrister and solicitor who drew up an agreement of separation between the Colebournes. Sid refused to sign the papers until Vera agreed to sign over custody of Hilda. This she reluctantly did and then moved into a room on Pandora Street, supplementing her work at the Crystal Garden by cleaning people's houses. Neighbours told police that Sid would frequently turn up drunk at the house, threatening to shoot her if she didn't return to him. Sid also refused to let her see Hilda, so Vera returned to the lawyer the following September to try to force Sid to let her see her daughter. When she found out that Hilda had been taken to the hospital three times during her absence, she went back to her husband. That had been at the end of January, two months before his death.

Sid bought a gun and told Vera that if she left him again, he would shoot her because he wasn't going to be humiliated in front of the neighbours. She was forbidden to visit her lawyer's office. He said she was going to pay for leaving him and that Vera's father would never testify against him in court because he would "receive a bullet."

Vera told Chief Syme that Sid had been angry on the night of his death because he thought 10:30 was too early to go home, especially while he was drinking with his buddy and having a good time. But little Hilda was tired and needed to go to bed. When they got home, Vera put Hilda to bed, and then Sid wanted to have sex with her. When she told him no, because she had a bad pain in her side, he hit her in the abdomen with his fist. He swore at her and then pressed his gun against her neck, repeating that if she tried to leave him again he would kill her and her father.

Sid's abusive behaviour continued to escalate, and Vera had had enough. She decided she would take the gun to a neighbour's house and telephone the Oak Bay police. She climbed back into bed and managed to get the gun from under her husband's pillow without waking him. She crawled out across the bed holding her daughter in one arm. When she was halfway across the bed, Hilda kicked out with one of her feet. The gun went off, and Vera fainted. She came to and called out to Sid, but he didn't answer. She remembered hearing a dripping sound, she said, but terrified, she gathered up her daughter in a quilt and tossed the gun in a hole in the chimney to hide it from Sid.

She threw the contents of a tin of paint on the top of the steps and left another tin on the verandah. If Sid woke up, she would tell him that someone had tried to steal the paint. Vera denied placing her husband's wallet in a roasting pan in the kitchen or hiding the jewellery box in the cupboard. She said that her husband often hid their valuables but didn't tell her where. She told police that she'd pulled the main light switch as they were leaving the house when Hilda started to cry. Vera didn't know her husband was dead until police told her three hours later.

Vera apologized to Chief Syme for telling the story about the man with the flashlight and said she would never have lied if she'd known that her husband was dead. She was terrified of him, but she had not meant to kill him.

Vera was charged with murder and her trial was set for the following October; in the meantime, she remained in jail. Hilda became a footnote to the tragedy—the only mention of her was that she had been placed with friends.

On October 17, the public galleries were full for the first day of Vera Colebourne's trial.[13] She had spent more than seven months behind bars. She pleaded "not guilty" to the murder of her husband. The jury of twelve men heard from fifteen witnesses. Vera's defence lawyer Richard Lowe built a case showing a frightened, abused woman who killed her husband in a tragic accident.

Vera told the court that she'd visited the office of Dr Hermann Robertson two weeks before the shooting for pains in her lower abdomen, where Sid had hit her, and again just over a week later when Sid hit her in the face and left her with a bruised lip. Other witnesses told police that they had seen Vera with a bruised face and black eye a few weeks before the shooting. Rose Otley, who had worked briefly as a housekeeper for the Colebournes, said she'd been fired when she threatened to tell police that Sid kept a gun in the house. Norah Youlden told of visiting the Colebourne home shortly before the shooting and telling Sid off for using "filthy, disgusting language" in front of his wife and child. She said that he shrugged his shoulders, laughed, and said, "he would like to carry her out of the house in a box."

Prosecutor M.B. Jackson tried his best to argue that the shooting was premeditated and painted a picture of a woman who killed her husband after years of abuse, then lied to cover it up. Realizing that the jury was sympathetic to her plight, Jackson tried another angle. He called up William Jones, the court usher, to the witness box. Jackson cocked Sid Colebourne's revolver and threw it on a chair. He knocked it across a table and finally dropped it on the floor. He asked Jones to repeat his actions. Fortunately for the jury, judge, and audience, the weapon did not fire.

---

13 Two days before the start of the trial, Victoria Police Chief John Syme, fifty-seven, shot and killed himself. Syme was found in the bushes in an area now known as Finnerty Gardens. Sergeant Reston was made the new police chief.

Lowe then called witnesses to prove that the revolver could be discharged without a direct pull on the trigger. A firearms expert named Frederick Butterfield described the tests he'd made with the revolver at the Colebourne home and told the court that it was an old, dangerous weapon that was easy to fire and could quite possibly have accidentally discharged.

A letter of commendation is sent to Chief Foster from the District of Oak Bay for the forensic work Vance did on the Colebourne case. *Courtesy of the Vance family*

When Inspector Vance took the stand, Lowe asked him to confirm that even if Vera had set off the gun accidentally, the results would have been fatal for Colebourne: "Assuming a gun was under the deceased's pillow, and his wife was on the bed alongside of the child, and Mrs Colebourne endeavoured to get the gun, and the gun went off accidentally, would what you state be consistent with the facts?" asked Lowe. "Yes," replied Vance.

The jury could not reach a verdict. The prosecution immediately called for a new trial, to begin eleven days later, on Halloween. At the end of the second trial, Mr Justice Fisher's charge to the jury lasted for more than three hours. He told them that they had two choices; either they found Vera guilty of murder or they found her not guilty. If they

Crowds line the 2200 block of Cornwall Street as they wait to catch a glimpse of King George VI and Queen Elizabeth in May 1939. *Vancouver Archives 6-139*

thought Sid Colebourne's death was accidental, they had to acquit Vera.

"There is no evidence of provocation under our code which in some cases would allow a verdict of manslaughter," he said. "The prisoner does not have to prove the killing was accidental. There is a great deal of circumstantial evidence in this case."

This time there was no doubt. The jury deliberated for one hour and thirty minutes and found Vera not guilty. Judge Fisher ordered her discharged from custody.

It's not known what happened to Hilda, but Vera married seventy-one-year-old John Rawlinson in 1949. John, a plumber by trade, ran the Ajax Tools and Curios store. He died four years later, and Vera continued to live in the Victoria area until her death in 1995 at age eighty-nine.

Vance returned to Vancouver where he was named Royal Analyst for the upcoming visit by King George VI and Queen Elizabeth. The royal couple and their entourage were travelling by Canadian Pacific Railway from Quebec City to Vancouver between May 17 and June 15, 1939. Vance was put in charge of inspecting everything from cream and fresh figs to smoked salmon, ducklings, lamb, and calves' brains destined for consumption by the royals.

Their visit ended just months before the outbreak of World War II.

All-female jury on the steps of the Vancouver Courthouse, 1929. *Vancouver Archives 99-1924*

Even though women had lobbied hard for the right to sit on a jury and won that right in December 1922, it wasn't unusual to see all-male juries, and that was certainly the case for both of Vera Colebourne's trials and the inquest into the death of her husband. Women were discouraged from sitting on juries for murder cases, and the law gave them an easy out. Until British Columbia passed the Jury Amendment Act in 1964, if chosen for jury duty, women would be notified by registered mail and given fifteen days in which to refuse, no questions asked.

In 1945, the year before this photo was taken at 906 Granville Street, the café was called the Good Eats and employed Olga Hawryluk. It changed hands in 1946 and was renamed the Esquire Café. *Vancouver Archives 1184-3378*

THE ENGLISH BAY MURDER

As for many Canadian families, World War II didn't leave the Vance family untouched. They lost their son Tom—thirty-year-old Major Thomas Cullen Brown Vance of the Seaforth Highlanders of Canada—on Christmas Eve 1943, when he was killed in action in Italy. He left behind a wife and baby daughter as well as his grieving parents, older brother, and two younger sisters.

But on May 7, 1945, Canadians celebrated the end of the war, the end of more than five years of fighting that cost the lives of 45,000 Canadian soldiers. "All through Canada, it was a day of celebration ... a day of thanksgiving, of fevered jubilation," trumpeted the *Globe and Mail*. "People went slightly mad, filled the streets with teeming paper, marched arm-in-arm, blew horns, kissed people they had never seen before. People went to church and prayed and cried."

In 1945, the population of Vancouver was just shy of 317,000. The city's West End—now dense with high-rises—was filled with single-family houses, and the tallest building was the eight-storey Sylvia Court Hotel. On the surface, life seemed simple and straight-laced, especially on Sundays when the city shut down because the Lord's Day Act prohibited business transactions on the Sabbath. That meant no movies, no sports events, and most certainly no booze. Nightclubs like the Commodore Ballroom or the Cave were not licenced, and if you wanted a hard drink you smuggled in a bottle, put it under the table, paid exorbitant prices for a mixer, and hoped that the police didn't raid the joint and confiscate your booze. If you just wanted a beer, you went to a beer parlour—women through one entrance, men through another, but never on Sundays.

The 1940s were a busy decade for bootleggers in Vancouver, and while alcohol testing still played a large role in Vance's work as city analyst, murder had begun to play an even bigger one. Just four months before the end of the war, Vance had been called in by the West Vancouver police to investigate a gruesome crime scene. Jennie Conroy, a twenty-four-year-old war worker from North Vancouver, was found with her head smashed in by a claw hammer. Her body had been dumped at the Capilano View Cemetery, and her murderer was never found.[14] And just five days before armistice, twenty-three-year-old Vancouverite Olga Hawryluk had been beaten to death and her body dumped in the waters of English Bay. Coincidentally, Olga, like Jennie, had worked at the North Vancouver shipyards during the war, and it's possible they knew each other.

Olga Hawryluk was born in Poland, grew up in the Peace River country at Harmon Valley, Alberta, and moved to Vancouver in 1941. She left her job at the shipyards and moved to Port Mellon on the Sunshine Coast for a short time, but at the time of her murder she was renting a room on Nelson Street in the West End and working as a cashier at both the Empire Café on West Hastings and at the Good Eats Café on Granville Street. Olga was an attractive young woman, and her co-workers described her as a quiet girl who didn't go to parties and didn't drink.

On May 2, 1945, Olga finished her shift at the Empire Café at 2:30 in the morning and left with her co-worker Dorothy Fornwald. The women walked up Granville Street; Dorothy went into Malcolm's Café. Olga told her she was going to go straight home, but she stopped in at the Good Eats Café. May Chalmers was working that night. She later remembered that Olga came in around 3:00 a.m. and took a seat on a counter stool near the front door. May noticed that she had been followed

---

14   Jennie's story is part of *Cold Case Vancouver: The City's Most Baffling Unsolved Murders* (Arsenal Pulp Press, 2015).

in by a tall, dark-haired man dressed in a grey coat and hat. He had very blue eyes, and May was sure he'd been drinking. Olga clearly didn't know him and she heard Olga tell him to "go away." May asked the man if he wanted something to eat and when he said no, she told him to get out of the café. He left but waited near the front door. "I didn't trust him," said May at the inquest.

Olga ordered a cup of coffee from May. She chatted to the staff for a few minutes and then started talking to a soldier who was sitting on the stool next to her. "The conversation was quite friendly. He seemed jolly," May said.

Rose Uron, the cashier on duty at the Good Eats that night, said that she heard the soldier ask Olga out, and Olga refused to go. When he tried to pay for Olga's coffee, Rose told him that Olga would take care of her own bill. Rose thought they were going to leave together, and she suggested that Olga have another cup of coffee. Olga didn't want more coffee but went to check the timesheets to see when her shift started the next day.

Lila Rogers chatted with Olga when she went into the kitchen. "She turned around to me and started to talk about her experience of this civilian and the soldier," said Lila. "She mentioned to me, rather laughingly, about being followed by a civilian up Granville Street and that she came into the café to get rid of him. She had a cup of coffee and said something like, 'After I got rid of the civilian, I sat beside the soldier, and he was pestering me for some time.'"

Rose said she asked Olga to wait in the café for a little while before heading home, but Olga told her she would be fine and left. Rose said that while Olga was bothered by the civilian who had followed her into the café, she seemed comfortable with the soldier. He had also probably been drinking, said Rose, but was in a happy mood, and she had the impression that Olga may have known him.

The next day, the front-page headlines detailed the murder of Olga Hawryluk, and Vance, once again, was part of the story.

In the early hours of May 2, the residents and guests of the English Bay Mansions on Bidwell Street woke up to the sounds of a woman screaming. Alice Wilson remembered hearing nine screams at exactly 4:48 a.m. and a "hammering—just like somebody chopping wood." The noise of the blows continued even after the screams had died out, she said.

Georgina Robinson and her daughter Hazel were in Vancouver staying at the English Bay Mansions when they were woken by a woman screaming, "Help me! Help me! God help me!" The two women threw on some clothes, and Hazel grabbed a flashlight. Georgina Robinson had a heart condition, so Hazel told her to take her time. Meanwhile, she dashed down to the beach, just across Alexandra Park.

"I had only been to English Bay Beach once before, and I didn't know my way down there very well. As I ran down the steps, I played my flashlight on the sand, then I shone it to the edge of the water and it outlined a man's head and shoulders. He had been right down on the water's edge. And just on the instant that I saw him, Mother came to the top of the beach and called, 'Hazel, do you see?'" and I said, 'Yes, I see him.'"

Hazel saw that the man was wearing a military uniform. Her first thought was that he had come down to the beach to investigate the screams. "Mother called to him and she asked him if he had heard a woman crying "'God help me.' He did not answer, and she called [to] him again, I cannot say how many times, and he finally answered 'No.'"

The fearless Hazel ran after the soldier and shone her flashlight in his face. He turned away from her and walked quickly down Beach Avenue. "I could not catch up to him and suddenly realized I would not know what to do even if I did catch up," said Hazel. She waved down a car driven by Russell Lutz, who told her he had seen the soldier

The English Bay mansions on Bidwell Street. *Eve Lazarus photo, 2017*

cross in front of his car near Denman Street, heading in the direction of the Burrard Bridge. Lutz drove off to notify police.

When Hazel returned to the beach, she and her mother followed a trail of blood on the sand where a body had apparently been dragged down to the water. They could see a woman's body lying face-down in the water about two feet (six metres) from shore. "I ran up, waded into the water, it was not very deep, caught hold of the shoulder and pulled the head and shoulders out of the water," said Hazel. The woman was wearing a black fur coat, a tan suit, gloves, a beret, and pumps. "Her face was horribly bruised and the forehead bashed in. She had no pulse," said Hazel.

Detectives George Pinchin and Neil McDonald arrived at the crime scene to find several people already gathered there. A man named Tom Slattery joined them and helped pull the body out of the water. As Tom looked around, he found two four-foot (1.2 metres) pieces of bloodstained cedar driftwood lying in the sand at the water's edge on either side of the body. Hazel showed the detectives the direction in which the soldier had gone and gave a description of him. He was about five-foot-eight (172 cm), she said, and because he wasn't wearing a hat, she'd noticed his dark, wavy hair. Pinchin went back to his car radio and called in the information.

The detectives took charge of the pieces of driftwood and searched the beach where they found a packet of Du Maurier cigarettes, a small bottle of perfume, two crumpled tissues stained with crimson lipstick, a lipstick case, a soldier's cap, and a bunch of keys that were later identified as Olga's. Police also found a sealed envelope with the Empire Café stamp.

Less than an hour after the body was found, Sergeant Dave Shearer and Constable Oliver Ledingham saw a soldier walking down Drake Street near Granville Street. Ledingham asked him to take his right hand out of his pocket. He saw that the soldier's hand had several cuts. A nail on his index finger was broken, and it was covered with blood. The officers noted several red spots on his tunic and his right pant leg. Sand clung to his wet boots and trouser cuffs. He wasn't wearing a hat.

As Ledingham questioned the soldier, he could see that he'd been drinking. He reeked of booze, and his hands were filthy, "black almost." The officer had to ask the soldier his name and number a couple of times, and he asked him if he had been "on a party." The soldier admitted to this and said that he was returning to his room at the Astoria Hotel on West Hastings Street. The following day, this soldier, twenty-nine-year-old William Hainen, appeared at police court charged with murder. He was in the prisoner box for less than two minutes. The *Province* described him as "unmoved and expressionless."

William Hainen was a stocky five-foot-eight and a former hard rock miner. When Vance arrived to examine him five hours after his arrest, the soldier still reeked of liquor. Vance took samples of charcoal and sand from Hainen's hair and hands. Vance was given Hainen's tunic, trousers, shirt, black tie, and damp black shoes and socks for analysis, as well as the cap and two pieces of driftwood found on the beach. He extracted two ounces (fifty-seven grams) of sand from Hainen's left shoe and found it matched the sand on the beach and on the cap that had been picked up by the detectives. Hainen's right trouser leg had similar sand stuck to it as well and was stained with blood. Vance proved that it was of the same blood type as Olga's, Group A, which belonged to forty percent of the population. The blood on the driftwood was also Group A. Because the driftwood was wet and had been handled by multiple people, there were no usable fingerprints found.

Vance analyzed the murdered woman's stomach contents, blood, and urine, and found no trace of either alcohol or drugs. A swab from her vaginal canal showed no evidence of sexual assault. Vance examined Olga's battered head and found her hair matted with blood, sand, and wood charcoal. The charcoal was the same as he found on the bloodstained pieces of driftwood and on Hainen's hands and in his hair.

In a line-up a few days after Olga's murder, May, Rose, and Lila all identified William Hainen as the soldier they had seen talking to her and leaving the café shortly before her murder.

On May 1, 1945, William Hainen got up around noon still hungover from a party held in his room until 4:00 that morning. He washed down some toast with half a mickey of rye, then he went to a beer parlour near his hotel and downed several beers. Later he met up with his sister Kathleen and her friends at another downtown tavern, where he drank more beer. The group took a cab to a café at Boundary and Hastings, picking up two bottles of rye along the way. After dinner they went to a supper club on East Hastings where they drank some more and danced. William left around 1:30 a.m. He took his unfinished bottle of rye and headed to the Good Eats Café for some food.

Not surprisingly, William had little memory of the night. At his trial he said: "There was a girl sitting with a civilian. I offered them a drink—I thought they had one. My next recollection was going down an alley or street. I must have had a bottle with me. After that we must have been going over a grassy boulevard. Then a fight started. The next thing, I fell on the ground. I don't know whether it was a ditch or what." He said the next thing he remembered was being arrested by police.

When Hainen was shown a picture of Olga he said that he knew her to see her, but didn't know her personally. It's possible that Olga and Hainen were acquainted. Hainen was staying at the Astoria Hotel on West Hastings across the road from the Empire Café, and it's likely he ate some of his meals there. "I certainly did not kill Olga Hawryluk," he said.

Angelo Branca,[15] who would later be appointed as a judge of the BC Supreme Court, was Hainen's defence lawyer. The eyewitness testimony identifying Hainen as the soldier seen at the beach after the murder was so strong that Branca decided a defence of unproven identity was hopeless. When he found out about the staggering amount of booze that Hainen had consumed on the day leading up to the murder, he advised Hainen that his best chance was to plead guilty and argue that he'd had so much to drink that he was incapable of forming the intent to kill. This way, he thought, his client would

---

15 Branca had defended sixty-three people on murder charges during his career, and only one, Domenico Nassa, received the death penalty in 1928. Branca had no quibble with that decision, but he didn't think Hainen deserved to hang.

get a verdict of manslaughter and escape the death penalty. Branca established that Hainen drank a thirteen-ounce (385-mL) bottle of rye at noon, twenty-four to thirty beers and an indeterminate amount of rum between 2:00 and 8:00 p.m., fifteen beers between 9:30 p.m. and 11:00 p.m., and more than half a bottle of rye afterwards.

Hainen came to court smartly dressed in a tweed sports jacket and brown trousers and looking nothing like the drunken soldier at the Good Eats. Thirty-three witnesses were called, including Dr Creighton, who'd done the autopsy. He testified that Olga had been so badly beaten that her brain was exposed. Her eyes were blackened, her jaw broken, and all her teeth knocked out from repeated blows from the driftwood.

The defence fell flat when the prosecutor convinced the jury that while he may have consumed a massive amount of alcohol, the fact that he beat Olga to death with repeated blows, placed the body where it would be carried away by waves, and tried to avert his face when approached by Hazel Robinson all showed intent.

Hainen explained that the blood stains on his clothes were from the cuts on his hands, although Vance had established that they were the same blood type as Olga Hawryluk's. Hainen's inability to explain how the charcoal—which matched that on Olga's battered body—got on his hands and in his hair also swayed the jury. Prosecutor Whiteside made a dramatic closing statement when he asked the jury for a murder conviction and said: "This was the sort of crime Jack the Ripper was guilty of. I do not think there is a doubt in anyone's mind that the accused committed the crime."

The jury deliberated for under three hours before coming back with a guilty verdict and a strong recommendation for mercy. Branca fought the verdict all the way to the British Columbia Court of Appeal. But the defence that his client was so drunk he could not form intent held no sway with the appellate court either. William Hainen was executed at Oakalla Prison Farm on October 20, 1945, just as other soldiers were arriving home from the war.

These soldiers now found they were competing for jobs and housing with the more than 20,000 people who flooded into the city from all over Canada in search of work. By 1946, 600 homeless, unemployed war vets occupied the second Hotel Vancouver.

Many of Vancouver's young men who were too young to fight in the war, and unable to find work, formed into "hoodlum gangs" where the average age was eighteen. The youth were good at steering clear of police, members were rarely identified, and their crimes were becoming increasingly serious. Police believed that an organized crime ring was recruiting boys (as young as thirteen) and using them to rob military depots and armouries and then using the stolen guns in robberies around the Lower Mainland.

GUN BATTLE AT FALSE CREEK FLATS

Shortly before noon on Wednesday, February 26, 1947, police received an anonymous tip that the Royal Bank at Renfrew and First Avenue was about to be robbed. Constable William Smith was the first to arrive at the branch, and when the three would-be robbers saw his police car they aborted the holdup and took off, with Smith in pursuit. The car chase tore through the streets of East Vancouver. At one point, Smith caught up and tried to ram the speeding car with his police car, but the robbers drove up on the sidewalk and got away. By this time, other police cars were closing in on the area and the three men dumped the stolen car at Kitchener and Nanaimo Streets and fled on foot through the Lord Nelson Elementary School grounds.

Detective Sergeant Percy Hoare and his partner Detective George Kitson were the first to reach the stolen car. Kitson got out and stayed with it while Hoare rushed toward the school, joining three other police cars that had moved in on the neighbourhood.

Arnold Montgomery was on his way to his grade six class with friends when they saw three older teens walking toward the Great Northern Roundhouse at Clark Drive and Grandview. When the boys were stopped and questioned by Detective Hoare, they gave him a description of the young men. Hoare told them to get in the police car. Arnold jumped in, but his two friends didn't want to be seen in a "cop car." As Hoare and Arnold drove down Charles Street, Hoare saw three men walking about a block from Clark Drive heading toward the False Creek Flats. One had a white package under his arm and another was wearing red.

"There was absolutely nothing suspicious about their actions," Hoare said later. "They never looked around, and never hurried. I was not particularly suspicious, but there was that red sweater, and the white parcel had caught my interest."

By the time Hoare arrived at the Roundhouse, officers Charles Boyes and Oliver Ledingham had already left their car and were heading to the spur track to try and intercept the young men. Hoare told Arnold to stay in the car, and he went to join the two officers.

Hoare saw Officers Ledingham and Boyes catch up to the three suspects. Ledingham took out his badge. The boys stopped and looked, but showed no sign of trouble. The three young men and the two officers turned and started making their way toward Hoare. Hoare asked one of the young men his name, but received no reply. He addressed all of them: "Who are you three fellows anyway?" Then the wind blew open one of the boys' coats, and Hoare saw the butt of a handgun sticking out of his black overalls. The detective grabbed the fully loaded .38 calibre revolver from seventeen-year-old William Henderson.

Before the officers could search the other young men, all hell broke loose when all three of them took off in different directions. Harry Medos and Doug Carter fired their guns: Medos shot Boyes through the heart before the officer had time to draw his weapon. Ledingham managed to get off one shot before he took a bullet to the chest. Carter fired six rounds, hitting Hoare in the leg. Hoare fell to the ground face first as a shot narrowly missed his head. As Hoare tried to reach his hand into his shoulder holster to get his gun, Medos fired another shot through his left shoulder. "There were several shots fired in quick succession," Hoare said later. "I knew they meant to kill us."

Hoare saw Medos and Carter running away separately. The left-handed officer took his gun in his uninjured right hand, aimed, and hit Carter in the leg. He fell. Then Carter got up and started to run

False Creek Flats in 1966, much the same as it was in 1947. The area was 450 acres and was bounded by the Great Northern Way, Main Street, Prior Street, and Clark Drive. *Vancouver Archives 780-502*

away and Hoare fired again, this time bringing him down permanently.

Next Hoare took aim at Medos and hit him in the leg too. Medos fell to the ground, but was able to get up again and continue on. Henderson joined Medos, and they ran for their lives through the False Creek Flats trying to lose police in the maze of boxcars and shunting locomotives.

Three female employees from Custom Packers saw the teens come over the crest of a hill from the False Creek Flats, and Medos waved his gun at them. As they ran around the corner of the building, Medos unsuccessfully tried to break into a locked coupe, and then came across an unlocked United Delivery Company truck. The truck belonged to Marcel Chapotelle, who was making a delivery nearby. When he saw Medos getting inside his truck, Chapotelle ran up, pulled open the door, asked the ashen-faced, bleeding young man what the hell he thought he was doing, and told him to get out of his truck. Medos pointed his gun at Chapotelle and said, "Help me get this thing started or I'll blow your brains out." Instead of answering, Chapotelle slammed the door in his face and ran around to the back of the truck. "Another man [Henderson] was across the street, holding a gun against his hip. I thought, 'This is where I get it.' I ran and started yelling for a phone." Medos got out of the truck, and he and Henderson ran through a vacant lot.

Detective Charles Geach was the first officer to reach the truck. He looked inside and could see that the front seat was saturated in blood. Chapotelle showed him the way the two young men had gone. They came across a brown tweed jacket, matching pants, a brown hat, and a blue shirt that had been tossed in some bushes in the vacant lot, then followed a trail of blood to the back of 647 East Sixth Avenue.

Geach kicked in the door to the basement and found Henderson hiding behind the chimney. He had changed from a green sweater into a white sweatshirt to disguise his appearance. "He put his hands over his head and said, 'Don't shoot. I will come out.'" Geach searched him and found he wasn't carrying a gun. By this time, other officers had reached the house and found Medos, still wearing his red sweater, slumped unconscious and bleeding in a dark corner of the basement. There was blood on the floor and a nickel-plated Iver-Johnson revolver rolled up in a bundle of clothing. Police also found Henderson's discarded green sweater with a pocket full of extra ammunition for his Smith & Wesson and a brown silk stocking that he'd planned to use in the bank holdup. Henderson told the detectives: "They can't blame me for shooting him; they took my gun away from me."

More than 100,000 people stood ten deep along Burrard and Georgia Streets for the funeral of officers Boyes and Ledingham at St. Andrew's Wesley Church. The men had been partners in prowler-car duty for

An overhead view of Burrard and Georgia Streets for the funeral of officers Boyes and Ledingham in 1947. *Vancouver Public Library 42982*

a month. They were noted as "outstanding" young officers.

The slain officers might have survived, Chief Mulligan said, had they frisked the boys for weapons when they first approached them. After their deaths, Chief Mulligan established a training program for police officers through the RCMP's facilities in Regina, Saskatchewan, and made it police policy to search anyone suspected of a criminal offence.

Just two days before the shooting, Police Chief Walter Mulligan told reporters that the "gloves were off" in a war against city crime. Over the next forty-eight hours, the *Vancouver Sun* reported, Vancouver experienced seven burglaries, two holdups, two attempted robberies, and nineteen thefts.

It was imperative that Mulligan sort out the recent shooting at False Creek Flats as soon as possible—and that's where Inspector Vance came in. Vance would need to determine who fired the weapons that killed three men and wounded two others. All of the evidence—guns, bullets, the blood-stained cushion from the truck, and the clothes—were sent to Vance for analysis.

When a gun is fired, small particles of lead shred off the bullet primer in its passage from the cylinder to the barrel and fly out onto the skin and clothing of the person holding the gun. The first thing Vance needed to do was examine the hands of those involved for gunshot residue; one of the most important aspects of the trial, at

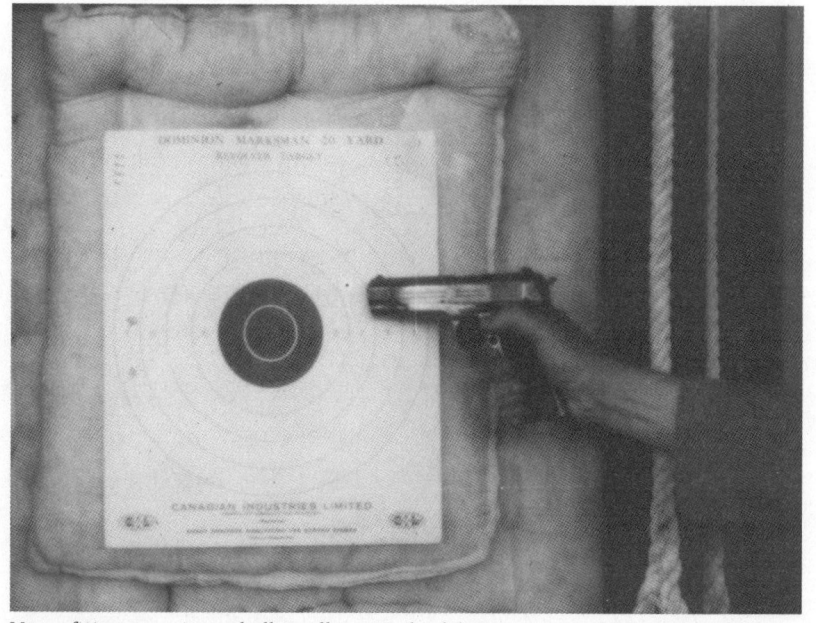

Vance firing a gun into a bullet collector in his lab to compare against a spent bullet. *Courtesy of the Vance family*

least for seventeen-year-old Henderson, would hinge on whether he took place in the shooting. Hoare testified that he had taken the gun from the teen before the shooting started, but several witnesses, including Chapotelle, swore that they had seen him with a gun. When Vance swabbed Henderson's hands at police headquarters, he found no traces of gunpowder on his hands, corroborating the boy's story that he had not fired a gun that day.

At Vancouver General Hospital, Vance swabbed Medos' hands and found residue. His right hand tested positively for nitrates, indicating that he had recently fired a gun. When Vance examined Carter's hands in the morgue, both tested positive for nitrates, indicating he'd also fired a gun. The right hand of Officer Ledingham had nitrate traces, which confirmed that he was able to get off a shot before he died, but there were no traces of nitrates on the hands of Officer Boyes.

In the lab, Vance examined the clothes the three young men were wearing at the time of the shooting and those taken from the house on Sixth Avenue where they'd been apprehended. He also examined the clothing of the two dead police officers. He didn't find any powder marks or burns on their bodies, and the clothing showed no indications of powder. It meant that the guns that killed them had not been fired at close range. Vance took the guns and the bullets to a miniature firing range in the lab. He placed a sheet of paper in front of several heavy layers of felt and fired the bullet into a collection device.

As Vance explained to a reporter, no two guns are exactly the same, even when they are manufactured in the same plant and on the same machine. "The grooves and lands of the bore are different. In the manufacturing process, the drill that is used to produce the bore never leaves exactly the same impression. The revolving drill always leaves a different 'scratch' or stops at a different point, and this impression is transferred to the bullet as it whirls through the bore," he said. "We have instruments so exact that we can tell by examining the spent shells whether the bullets were fired from a certain gun."

Vance examined the police-issue .38 calibre H&R revolver that was taken from the holster of Officer Boyes and confirmed that it had not been fired. He fired test bullets from the other revolvers and then compared them to the spent bullets found at the crime scene using a comparison microscope. He examined the .38 calibre bullets taken out of Carter's right buttock and chest and noted that both were fired from Hoare's Colt .38 calibre Army Special. The bullets removed from the bodies of Ledingham and Boyes came from the Iver-Johnson .38 revolver that belonged to Medos. The bullets taken out of Hoare's leg and shoulder were both from the 44.40 calibre Colt Frontier Six-Shooter that Carter was holding when he died.

Harry Medos and Bill Henderson were jointly charged in the

Vance called this "gun printing." He used this machine to make an exact reproduction of the markings of the bore (interior) of a gun from which he could determine if a particular gun fired a particular bullet. *Courtesy of the Vance family*

murders of the two police officers, although they would be tried separately. Police said that Henderson and Medos were part of a Lower Mainland gang operation responsible for at least four recent bank holdups including an armed robbery.

Police had also picked up a young truck driver named William Faulder (Fats) Robertson the day after the shooting and held him on bail as a material witness. Robertson told of meeting Medos and Carter the day before the shooting to discuss the robbery, and the next morning he, Medos, Carter, and Henderson met for breakfast at the Aristocratic Café on Kingsway. Later investigation revealed that Robertson, who was suspected in several other robberies, was the anonymous caller who had tipped police off before the bank holdup. The four usually worked together; Robertson had been left out, and it was believed that he had phoned the police in revenge.

Eighteen-year-old Douglas Eldon Carter had a wife and five-

The Burrard Hotel at 712 Richards Street where Harry Medos and his girlfriend Mary Peterson were living at the time of the shootings. *Vancouver Archives 779-E09.35*

month-old baby. Friends told reporters that his wife had kicked Doug out of the house because of the shady company he was keeping. Doug's mother, Mae Carter, said she was glad her son was dead. "I'd rather jump into the inlet and die than see my boy face trial for murder," she said. "There are crooks on the loose in this town who've been in and out of jail and never go straight and all they do is teach younger lads their evil ways. It was only recently that Doug started going around with them. He was never in trouble with police before."

Medos's live-in girlfriend, Mary Magdalene Peterson, was the key witness for the prosecution. She told reporters that at least thirty members of the gang that Harry belonged to were "out to get her." She had met Harry just six weeks before the shootings at a lodge on Vancouver Island where she was working. He told her he was a bond salesman named Harry Johnson and was there "to cool off." When he left to go back to Vancouver, she went with him, and at the time of

Police Murderer Medos Loses Daring Escape Bid

Slayer, Hidden in Garbage Can, Discovered by Guard

Harry Medos, convicted killer of Prowler Officer Charles Boyes in February's False Creek flats gun battle, was foiled in an escape attempt from Oakalla Prison Farm at 8:10 a.m. today.

Warden John Milman said the 23-year-old convict was helped by two "trusties" of the prison.

Medos had hidden himself in a barrel of garbage being carried out of the area by the two other inmates.

Alertness of a prison guard brought him back to custody. Prison authorities will take "disciplinary action" against the two trusties.

APPEAL DUE

His appeal from conviction on the murder charge is to be heard in Victoria Sept. 9. He had previously been sentenced to hang July 28.

Warden Milman told The Vancouver Daily Province this morning that the slayer was being carried in the barrel to a dump in the prison yard by two trusties. He feed was partly covered by papers and garbage.

SOON CAUGHT

When the guard spotted him, he jumped out and started to run, but was caught after a short chase.

"It is a good thing the officer discovered him. He might have been lucky enough to get away with it," Warden Milman declared.

"But he didn't have much chance after he jumped out of the barrel. He was still inside the grounds, and would not have got very far."

The can would have been taken to the main dump within

garbage removed later by truck.

The warden said no charges can be laid against an attempted escape such as Medos tried. It would have to be successful before such action could be taken.

"We won't do anything except keep a tighter watch on the man," he declared.

Medos made a previous escape from Oakalla in August, 1946, when he was serving a one-year term for car theft and entering with intent to steal.

He was recaptured after two days' freedom.

In the February gun battle—in which two policemen and one youth were killed—Medos suffered serious wounds.

He was confined to General Hospital, under police guard, for about a month after the shooting.

SENTENCED TO DIE

Then, in May, he was convicted of the killing and sentenced to hang by Mr. Justice Manson.

A few days later, his accomplice in the shooting, 17-year-old William Henderson, was also convicted by the same judge. Charges covered only the murder of Prowler Officer Boyes, although Prowler Officer G. O. Ledingham and another bandit suspect also were killed in the

HARRY MEDOS
Escape foiled.

Man Dies In Auto Collision

Special to The Daily Province

LANGLEY PRAIRIE — One man is dead and a woman is in hospital following an automobile collision at the corner of the Trans-Canada Highway and the Johnson Town Line Road, a mile east of Langley Prairie, at 9:15 Tuesday night.

Dead is Nick Friesen, 24, of Yarrow.

Mrs. Frank Martens of Yarrow is in fairly good condition in

Harry Medos. The *Province*, August 27, 1947.
Courtesy of the Vance family

the shootings they were living in a room at the Burrard Hotel on Richards Street.

Mary testified that on the night before the shootings, Bill Henderson, Doug Carter, and William (Fats) Robertson came to their room. "I thought a lot of Harry and didn't want to accuse him of anything I was not sure of, and I asked him if he really would hold up a bank. He said, 'If I don't tell you anything, you won't know anything.'"

Judge Alex Manson presided over Medos' trial. He told the jury that there was no chance of manslaughter; the shooting was cold-blooded murder, and it would be murder or nothing. The jury deliberated for thirty-seven minutes before finding Medos guilty. He was sentenced to hang. An hour before his execution, Medos told a guard on death row that he had a headache and wanted an aspirin. When the guard left to get him some medication, Medos took out a razor blade that he'd stashed under his mattress and slashed his wrists. Finding him barely alive, the prison doctor revived him, bandaged him up, and declared him fit for his 6:00 a.m. execution.

In his green tweed sport coat, shirt, and tartan tie, baby-faced Bill Henderson looked like he'd just stepped out of a high school classroom. Even before his trial started, the Crown had told reporters that they were considering applying to the Attorney General to reduce his charge from murder to "accessory after the fact." Henderson was convicted of

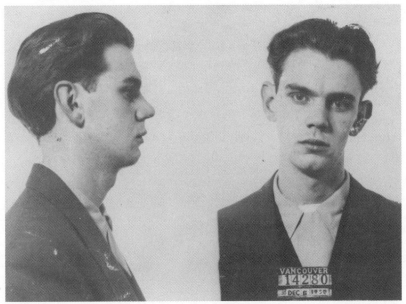

Mugshot of seventeen-year-old William Henderson in 1947. *Vancouver Police Museum* 2395

murder and sentenced to hang, but the sentence was overturned on appeal. In the end, he was acquitted of the murder and received five years for possession of a firearm.

In 1949, Chief Mulligan announced that "Vancouver police have ended their 'kid glove' policy" toward juvenile offenders and "instead of warnings, we're going to lay charges and eradicate the law-flaunting element." The following year, the VPD created the "Youth Guidance Detail" to stamp out juvenile delinquency.

Eleven days after the False Creek Flats shooting that claimed the lives of Officers Boyes and Ledingham, Vance was summoned to a Kitsilano apartment to check out the suspicious death of a young woman.

George Oliver Ledingham lived in the Kitsilano neighbourhood of Vancouver. Originally from Ontario, he was married with a thirteen-year-old son. Ledingham joined the force in 1935, the same year as Boyes. Outside of work and family, he liked to golf and fly fish, but his passion was  gardening, and he was known in the neighbourhood for the crops of gladioli and the tulips he cultivated in the yard of their little white bungalow.

English-born Charles Boyes had studied mechanical engineering and then served in the British Army in India for seven years before arriving in Vancouver in 1934. He joined the police force and had recently been promoted to the prowler-car detail. He lived in Vancouver's Point Grey  neighbourhood with his wife and six-year-old daughter. Boyes was known as a wizard with tools and often fixed the toys of the neighbourhood kids.

SPANISH FLY

1825 West 4th Avenue. *Eve Lazarus photo, 2017*

On March 9, 1947, seventeen-year-old Ruth Cooperman was found naked and lying dead across Jack Cooperman, her twenty-seven-year-old husband, in their Kitsilano apartment.

That morning, Ruth had phoned her father David Simons and told him she would be over to see him later that day. Around 3:00 p.m. she spoke to her sister Esther and brother-in-law Lloyd Tuffs, and told them she and Jack would come by for dinner. When the couple didn't arrive, the Tuffs weren't overly concerned. The plans were casual and Ruth and Jack had broken appointments before.

Meanwhile, other family members were trying to get in contact with the couple, and finding the line out of order, started to worry. About 8:00 p.m., Lloyd Tuffs dropped around to check on them. "I

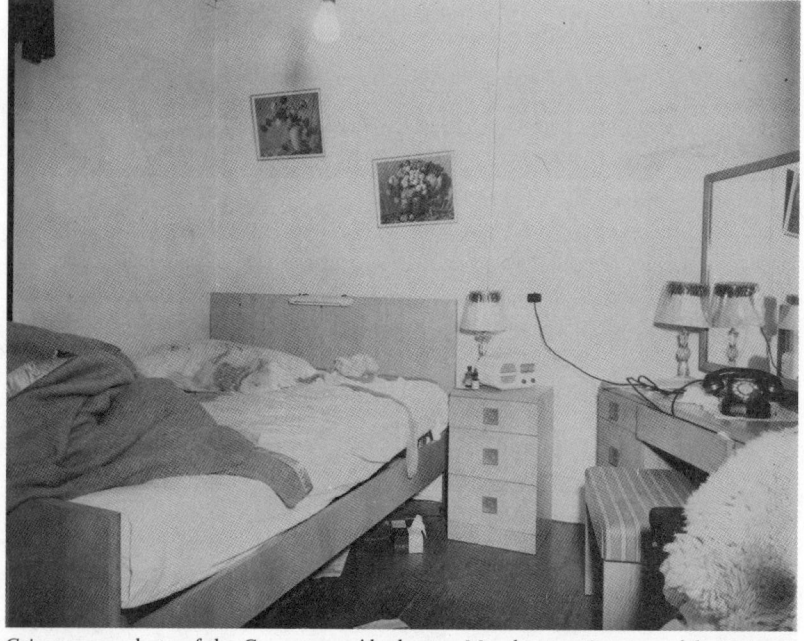

Crime scene photo of the Coopermans' bedroom, March 1947. *Courtesy of the Vance family*

hammered on the windows and doors and hammered and hammered with no response," he said. Tuffs broke into the apartment through the kitchen window. There was a light on in the bathroom and as he entered the bedroom he could see two naked bodies lying on the bed. He was embarrassed, he said, and stood at the door asking if they were all right. The only reply was a groan from Jack Cooperman. At this point, Jack's parents Harry and Sarah Cooperman and Ruth's parents David and Annie Simons arrived at the house. The scene in the bedroom was chaotic and confused.

Tuffs later said that his first thought was that they had had too much to drink. He found the bath full of unused water and vomit in the bathroom and bedroom. The phone had been knocked to the floor. Tuffs called for an ambulance, which arrived within minutes.

Ruth lay on her back, blood streaming from her mouth. The members of the inhalator squad gave her artificial respiration, but when the doctor arrived she was declared dead. Jack was rushed to Vancouver General Hospital.

Vance and Detective Percy Easler were summoned to the apartment, which was now officially a crime scene. Easler took photos while Vance had police gather up the bedclothes, vomit-stained pillow and bedsheet, a vaginal douche, a silver knife, and a brown paper bag containing the contents of a garbage bin. He also took to his lab salt and pepper shakers, what was left of a bottle of Four Roses bourbon and another of Imperial single malt, and a decanter of clear liquid.

Mystery Shrouds Bride's Death; Autopsy Fails to Reveal Cause

Mystery of death of 17-year-old Mrs. Ruth Cooperman and desperate illness of her 27-year-old husband, Jack, will not be solved until Police Scientist, Inspector J. F. C. B. Vance, completes analysis of samples of the woman's blood and stomach contents.

Autopsy held at noon proved fruitless, it is reported.

SAVED HUSBAND

The bride of seven months collapsed and died across her husband's body Sunday afternoon, after both were stricken in their honeymoon apartment at 1825 West Fourth, apparently food poisoning.

Her dying efforts apparently saved her husband's life.

Remains of a cake were found; are being analyzed.

An inhalator crew was unable to revive Mrs. Cooperman.

Jack Cooperman is in General Hospital, his condition fair. An ex-serviceman, he had been taking treatment at Shaughnessy Hospital for war wounds.

They lived at 1825 West Fourth.

(Continued on Page 2)
See POISON

MRS. RUTH COOPERMAN

Seventeen-year-old Ruth Cooperman shortly before her death. *Daily Province*, March 10, 1947. *Courtesy of the Vance family*

It looked like a case of severe food poisoning, especially after police learned that Ruth had been treated for vomiting and abdominal cramps the previous month. Vance suspected drugs were involved when he saw a box of Luxury chocolates in the room and six of the candies had their bases pushed in. At the hospital, police learned that vomiting whatever he'd ingested had probably saved Jack's life, but that his condition was critical; if he did survive, it would be several days before they would be able to interview him.

The autopsy of Ruth's body failed to reveal her cause of death. The city pathologist sent the sealed jars containing stomach contents, blood, and urine to Vance's lab. Vance began to test for and then eliminate dozens of different drugs and poisons until he could determine cause of death. He discovered that Ruth's stomach contents and the vomit on the pillow contained Cantharides; she had died from an overdose of that drug, known on the streets as "Spanish Fly." Made from the oil of a beetle, Cantharides was known for its purported aphrodisiac properties and its supposed ability to treat impotence. It was mostly used to stimulate animal breeding, was considered highly toxic to humans, and was difficult to obtain. After Vance's results were made public, the newspapers called it "the love drug."

Vance tested everything that was brought to the lab from the house. There was no trace of Cantharides in the chocolates or the liquids, and the cups and other dishes had been washed. The only evidence he found were a few fragments of the powder in a bottle that was marked "Tuinal," a drug used as a sedative in the 1940s.

The coroner announced there would be no inquest. David Simons, Ruth's father, was furious. He blamed his son-in-law for his daughter's death. Jack Cooperman, an ex-serviceman turned salesman,

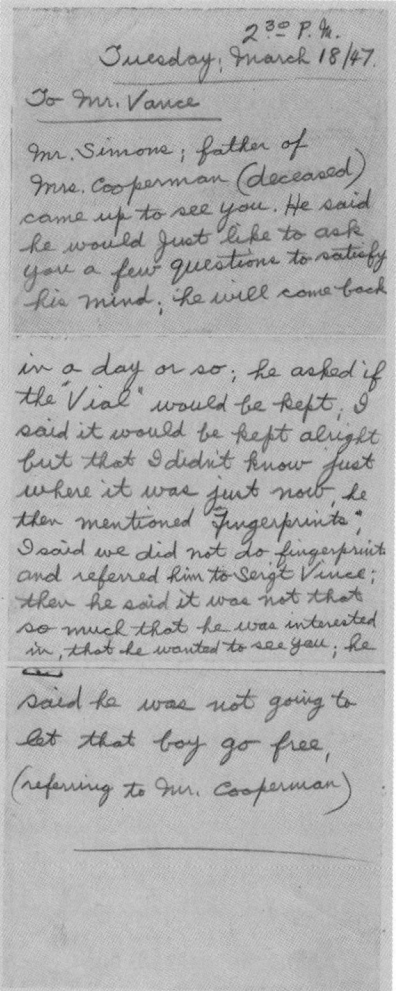

Note left for Vance on March 18, 1947 that David Simons, Ruth Cooperman's father, wanted to talk to him.
Courtesy of the Vance family

had successfully managed to deflect most of the blame onto his young wife. When Harry Cooperman, Jack's father, told Simons that Ruth had been the one to procure Spanish Fly, Simons, a former boxer, hit his old friend. Cooperman pressed charges, and Simons was later found guilty of assault and battery.

Simons wanted an inquest into his daughter's death and a chance to get at the truth. He wrote to toxicologists and pharmacologists at the University of Washington to search for information about aphrodisiac drugs. He harassed Vance, the police chief, the police commission, and the Attorney General's department for the next two years until finally, on April 14, 1949, he got his inquest and his daughter's body was exhumed.

Ruth Cooperman on her wedding day. *Vancouver Sun,* January 28, 1952. *Courtesy of the Vance family*

It was an emotion-filled day of dramatic accusations, denials, charges, and counter-charges. Had Jack given the drug to Ruth as an aphrodisiac, or did Ruth give the drug to Jack to stimulate potency because she so badly wanted a baby?

Harry Cooperman told the coroner that a few years back, Simons had shown him a little bottle and said, "That's good for stimulation." He called Simons "a chippy chaser" (a womanizer). Simons kept repeating the words "lying, lying" throughout Cooperman's testimony.

Jack told the jury that Ruth had been a "very good wife to him," but it was Ruth's character that was put on trial. Answering questions directed at him from the coroner, Jack said he hadn't known that Ruth was probably unable to have children because she had contracted salpingitis, an infection in the fallopian tubes often caused by a sexually transmitted disease such as gonorrhea. When asked by the coroner if he knew that she had "gone with men" previous to meeting him, Jack answered, "I had a good idea. I was pretty sure, but I never asked her and she never told me."

Jack told the jury that his wife must have drugged their coffee on the morning of her death. "I remember she brought the coffee into the bedroom and insisted I drink it. So I drank it. About fifteen minutes later, I got a terrific pain and I guess I passed out." Jack said he remembered that the coffee tasted terrible.

David Simons' lawyer, David Sturdy, objected heatedly several times. Eventually he asked to be excused, gathered up his papers, and walked out of the hearing protesting that "two years of my client's life are being frittered away."

David Simons, age fifty-one. *Daily Province*, January 29, 1952. *Courtesy of the Vance family*

The jury returned a verdict that the "death-dealing dose" of Cantharades "was administered by a person or persons unknown," and the coroner told Simons, "I would see a psychiatrist if I were you, because this whole thing has deteriorated your mentality. You don't think clearly now as you used to think when I first talked to you."

Simons remained convinced that Jack Cooperman, now called John Cooper, had poisoned Ruth, and the inquest's unsatisfying result seemed to have further unhinged him. For the next few years, he stalked his former son-in-law. Cooper, remarried, said that both he and his wife had received a number of calls threatening his life and that of his children. "I know [Simons] was making the calls, but I am unable to prove it," Cooper told a reporter.

On January 27, 1952, around 9:00 p.m., Cooper and his wife Laura were sitting in their car outside their apartment on McBride Boulevard

Photos of Jack ("John") Cooper and his second wife Laura point to the bullet holes in their car. *Vancouver Sun*, January 28, 1952. *Courtesy of the Vance family*

in New Westminster when a car pulled up beside them and an assailant pumped two shots into the driver's side door. One bullet pierced the car body just below the window, the other hit just beneath the door handle. Fortunately for the Coopers, the bullets were soft-nosed and didn't penetrate the car's exterior.

As the car with the shooter—a 1945 Pontiac sedan—pulled away with two men inside, Jack (now "John") gave chase. He managed to catch up to them several blocks away and tried to force their car into a ditch. At that point, John got a good look at Simons and was able to get the license number. The police soon apprehended the two men.

David Simons had gone to the old Jewish cemetery that morning to visit Ruth's grave. He stayed for a long time, growing increasingly despondent, then phoned his friend Tony Kostick and asked if he would drive him to New Westminster. Simons at first denied being the shooter, but when police demanded that he tell them where the gun was, he said, "You will never find the weapon." He told police that

Kostick knew nothing about his intentions. Kostick was released, and Simons was charged with attempted murder.

At his trial on May 7, Senator J.W. Farris and Nathan Nemetz, future chief justice of the Supreme Court, defended Simons. They argued that if Simons had fired the shots, it was not with intent to murder Cooper but rather to scare him into a confession of guilt for the death of his daughter.

Cooper was flippant and hesitant on the stand and did nothing to endear himself to either judge or jury. He said that he and his wife had received threats by letter and phone for the past two years, which stopped when Simons was arrested. None of the letters were produced in court. Simons was convicted of attempted murder with a strong recommendation for mercy by the jury. The gun was never recovered.

The case must have haunted Vance because the files that he took with him when he retired in 1949 included the original police report on Ruth's death and a list of items taken from the apartment, his notes on the case, crime scene photos, and newspaper clippings on the story up until 1952. In fact, he'd delayed his official retirement partly so that he could attend Ruth Cooperman's inquest in April of 1949. The inquest lasted for nine hours—the longest on record for one case—and the newspaper articles about it are interesting as much for what is missing as what was reported—information that involved Jack Cooperman's (John Cooper's) medical history and his relationship with Mrs Roland Constantine, a seventeen-year-old who called herself the "Black Widow."[16]

---

16   When I first ordered the record of the inquest from the BC Archives, it couldn't be found. Months later it turned up, but when I received it, more than twenty pages were missing. Text was redacted and several sections pertaining to Jack's medical condition, information about Ruth's connection to a Mrs Constantine with whom Jack later had an affair, and Ruth's background were omitted under the Freedom of Information and Protection of Privacy Act, Section 22 (a) and (h).

The Ruth Cooperman case wasn't the only one that Vance followed into his retirement. His personal files were filled with notes on the Walter Pavlukoff case, discussed in the next chapter, and contained every newspaper clipping about the robbery, murder, and ensuing manhunt, as well as notes in his own handwriting dated September 2, 1947, listing the evidence he had received.

People watching the Pacific National Exhibition parade along Hastings Street on August 25, 1947. It was the first one in six years and the largest in Vancouver's history. *Vancouver Archives CVA 180-1328*

MANHUNT

On August 25, 1947, an estimated 100,000 people stood along Georgia, Granville, and Hastings Streets waiting for the Pacific National Exhibition parade—the first one in six years (due to the war) and the largest in Vancouver's history. The parade kicked off at 10:30 in the morning. People were lined up five deep along the streets and hung out of office windows, while others had clambered up billboards or perched on top of trucks parked along the side streets. The crowd clapped and cheered as a hundred decorated floats rolled past, as well as Hugh Elmer's accordion band, the police, army, and air force bagpipe bands, the mounted police squad, and war veterans whose float had a grave, a cross, and a sign saying "Lest We Forget." There was excitement as Hollywood actor Allan Jones drove by, and the crowd even cheered for Chief Constable Walter Mulligan as the two-hour parade wound its way through city streets.

That morning, Walter Pavlukoff left his room at the Rancho Hotel on East Cordova. "Such a fine day," he said to Nell Millspaugh, the front-desk clerk, who knew him only as "a nice boy" called Walter Andrew who had stayed there for several weeks. Pavlukoff blended into the parade crowd on East Hastings, a Luger automatic pistol in his pocket.

Pavlukoff's parents had immigrated from Russia in 1907 and lived on Keefer Street in the East End where the family attended the Russian Orthodox Church and the kids went to Strathcona Elementary School. Pavlukoff spent his early years eking out a living at the logging camps along the coast. The rest of the time he lived at home with his mother.

The Pavlukoff family home at 2616 McGill Street in East Vancouver. *Eve Lazarus photo, 2017*

Pavlukoff was nineteen the first time he landed in jail in Chicago; he'd been convicted on five charges of robbery. After completing a five-year prison sentence, he was returned to Canada, and three weeks later received two years at the BC Penitentiary for armed assault with intent to steal. Within weeks of his release he was back in jail, serving another three years for robbery with violence. Shortly after his release he was again arrested, this time for illegal possession of a gun. When police searched him, they found a list with names of prominent citizens under the heading "Names I should know." "They have good jobs, nice homes, big cars, and smoke good cigars," he told the officers who arrested him. He called it a "sucker" list. Pavlukoff got another three years for possession of a weapon and was released from jail in November 1946.

Inspector Vance's first brush with the Pavlukoff family was in April 1934 when Walter's older brother Nick was arrested for robbing the London Grocery Store at Commercial and Venables. When detectives arrived at his home, they found a pair of men's trousers and an overcoat submerged in a tub of water. Vance found minute particles of sugar and burlap stuck to the clothing that were very similar to the sugar in the burlap sacks stolen from the store. Nick Pavlukoff received a nine-month prison sentence at Oakalla.

It's impossible to know what Walter Pavlukoff was thinking the morning he stood watching the PNE parade, but he didn't appear to be planning a bank robbery. In fact, his only planned act that afternoon was the purchase of a paper bag and a newspaper from George Chin, the owner of a grocery store near the Canadian Bank of Commerce at Broadway and McKenzie in Kitsilano. The bag was to be used for the cash, and the newspaper to shield his Slavic features. After that, his actions went from one tragic absurdity to another.

Sydney Petrie. *Vancouver Sun,* August 26, 1947. *Courtesy of the Vance family*

When Pavlukoff entered the bank a few minutes before its 3:00 p.m. closing time, there were still six customers and several staff inside. With the newspaper in front of his face, Pavlukoff poked customer John Stewart in the ribs with his gun and told him, "Get back against the wall and no funny work," and then said to the teller, "This is a stick-up. Don't give an alarm." He went to the back of the bank where his attention was caught by Sydney Petrie, the manager, who was taking a letter out of the typewriter.

Petrie had been with the Bank of Commerce for nearly forty years. He had stopped a robbery there in 1930, and was determined to do so again. As Pavlukoff moved toward him, the bank manager stood up and leaned forward, putting his shoulder under the heavy desk and pushing it at the gunman. Pavlukoff fired. The bullet passed through Petrie's abdomen, ricocheted off the floor, and then shattered a plate glass window at the front of the bank. Without

The Kitsilano branch of the Canadian Bank of Commerce in August 1947. *Vancouver Sun*, January 8, 1953. *Courtesy of the Vance family*

stopping to collect any money, Pavlukoff jumped over a counter and ran from the bank, dropping the paper bag in a crumpled heap on the counter as people screamed and flung themselves to the floor.

Robert Sowden, the bank accountant, rushed over to help Petrie. "Have you been hit, sir?" he asked him. Petrie said, "No, I don't think so," and crawled to the bank vault, got out the gun, and handed it to Sowden. Sowden turned and ran out of the office after Pavlukoff, calling to one of the tellers to tend to their boss. Sowden found Constable John McArthur sitting in his car near the bank writing a report. Sowden told him about the robbery, and the officer joined in the chase.

One of the bank customers ran to the grocery store next door and shouted, "It's a bank holdup; call the police!" He commandeered a car with two young men in it and sped off after the bank robber as he ran east on Broadway toward MacDonald. By now police had a description of Pavlukoff—about five-foot-ten, around thirty years old, with a slim build, sallow complexion, square jaw, deep-set pale blue eyes, dark hair, and wearing a fawn jacket and blue hat.

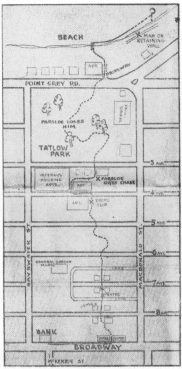

Back at the bank, paramedics were futilely trying to save Petrie's life. He died on the way to Vancouver General Hospital.

Pavlukoff ran through the back alleys of Kitsilano, jumped over fences, and dodged between houses. He dropped the gun's cartridge clip in a garden on Fourth Avenue where the homeowner saw him run through the yard and vault over the fence. He lost his blue fedora in Tatlow Park, scrambled down over a rock garden, and burst through a gate to the beach below Point Grey Road. Here he tore

Map of the chase through Kitsilano. *Vancouver Sun,* January 12, 1953. *Courtesy of the Vance family*

off his coat and vest, threw them in the reeds, and dashed across the beach toward Kits Point.

Police threw a road block up along Burrard Bridge and searched all eastbound traffic. More police commandeered boats from the Yacht Club to search along Kits Point and into False Creek. They searched until darkness forced them to stop. Pavlukoff had disappeared. He'd dodged a dragnet of more than a hundred armed police officers.

Meanwhile, the clothes, the hat with the initials W.P., the key, Luger, clip with four live rounds of ammunition, and the spent bullet found in the street outside the bank were tagged, bagged, and handed over to Inspector Vance for analysis and comparison.

While police were searching through the homes, rooming houses, hotels, and known criminal haunts in the downtown area and the East End, Sergeant Percy Hoare, hero of the False Creek Flats gun battle just six months earlier, and Detective Arthur Stewart were trying to identify the robber from the discarded clothing. The detectives spent the morning trying to trace the coat and vest through cloth wholesalers. Their investigation paid off when they reached Ormende Hall, sales manager for Kemp and Company, who told them the company had imported enough of the blue suit material from Australia to make sixty suits, and gave them a list of the tailors they supplied.

Hoare and Stewart hit the streets of Chinatown, checking tailors until they finally had some luck at their fifth call at the Wo On Co. tailors on East Hastings Street. Owner Dang Yee Gee's records revealed that he had sold a suit made from that material to a Walter Pavlukoff in November 1946, just a few days after his release from jail. The tailor showed the detectives a page from his book with the measurements for Pavlukoff and a piece of cloth from the suit material attached.

Gradually, other pieces of evidence began to turn up. On September 1, a gun with a live bullet in the chamber was found buried in the sand at Kitsilano beach. A few days later, a key to Room 47 at the Rancho Hotel was found.

Around this same time, the newspapers were filled with stories about the West Kootenay Doukhobors, a Russian religious sect known for their acts of dissent. The "Sons of Freedom" protested against compulsory schooling and anything that smacked of government intervention, including the registration of births, deaths, and marriages. They burned their homes and those of others, threw bombs, and marched naked through the streets. Reports of a "reign of terror by fanatical Doukhobor torch-raiders," as well as wife swapping were sharing front-page headlines with the manhunt for Walter Pavlukoff, described as "a sallow, shabbily dressed Doukhobor." While Pavlukoff was of Russian heritage, he was no Doukhobor.

For three days, it seemed that Pavlukoff had disappeared without a trace. And then on Thursday, August 28, Pat Richey, a prison guard at Oakalla Prison Farm, came home to his Surrey farm to feed his 130 chickens. His dog Laddie gave the alarm, and he looked out to see a man he recognized as Pavlukoff, a former inmate, trying to steal some eggs. Other reports came in from the area. A woman said she was walking down a lane when a man walking ahead of her jumped into the nearby bushes, and two teenage girls reported seeing a man in dirty brown clothes peer out of the bushes at them.

Walter Pavlukoff. *Vancouver Province* March 28, 1953. *Courtesy of the Vance family*

Armed police from all over Greater Vancouver converged in Surrey, and Vancouver Police Chief Walter Mulligan supervised the search and the sixty-man posse. It was the most intensive manhunt in Vancouver police history, with officers armed with rifles, automatics, sub-machine guns, sawed-off shotguns, and tear gas.

Road blocks were thrown up across all roads and bridges leading in and out of Surrey. A mug shot of Pavlukoff was published in the dailies for the first time on August 30. The photo led to new sightings, either real or imagined, and the chase proceeded south through Newton to the US border. Hundreds of acres of land, farms, and

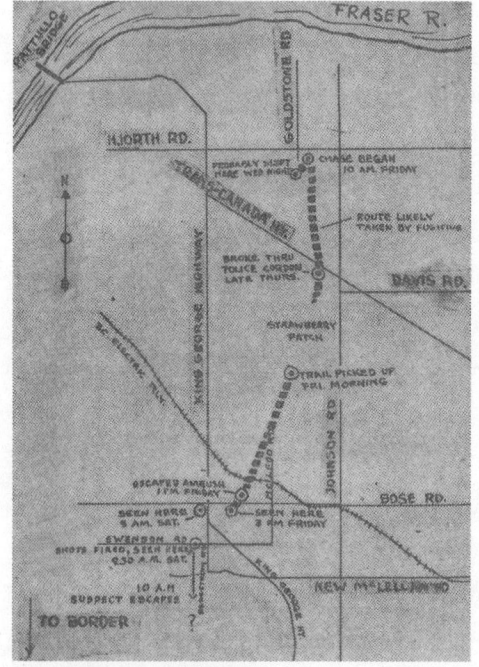

Map of the Surrey manhunt. *Vancouver Sun,* July 9, 1953. *Courtesy of the Vance family*

sheds were searched in a $10,000 manhunt that sent more than 200 hunters, trappers, and other civilians to join soldiers and police. But Pavlukoff wasn't to be found, and Mulligan called off the search.

But soon after, seventy-three-year-old Adam Tootell saw a photo of Pavlukoff in the newspaper. He told police that Pavlukoff had turned up at his shack by the CPR right-of-way in North Burnaby the day after the bank robbery. Pavlukoff asked him if he could split some wood in return for a meal. "He looked kind of decent to me so I gave him a meal," said Tootell. "He had lots of cigarettes so we sat around and smoked. He seemed like a nice fellow."

Tootell said he noticed that the heel of one of Pavlukoff's shoes was missing and the other one was loose. He gave him some boots and one of his old shirts. The clothes that Pavlukoff had left—a pair of battered, black Oxford shoes and a light-coloured blue shirt—were handed over to Inspector Vance to examine.

The summer of 1947 was Mulligan's first year as police chief, and police had plenty to keep them busy. The department was still reeling from the murder of officers Boyes and Ledingham in February, which the *Vancouver Sun* reported was just the "latest development in the all-out war between members of an apparently well-organized underworld, and fighting-mad city police."

Sydney Petrie would be one of six people murdered in Vancouver that year. In October, police dealt with the brutal murder of seven-year-old Roddy Moore on his way to school.[17] Roddy's murder didn't even rate a mention in the year-end police report. Vancouver was still in flux after the war. The city experienced a transit strike and a housing shortage. and squatters appeared in tents around the city or found abandoned shacks in isolated areas such as Tootell had done.

Over the years, there were many alleged Pavlukoff sightings, likely from people encouraged by the $5,000 reward put forward by the Canadian Bankers Association. But it wasn't until five-and-a-half years later that the RCMP got their man—the second on Canada's most wanted list.

In December 1952, William Moore, the manager of Pollock's Shoe Store on Toronto's Yonge Street, was in the North York police station when he noticed a wanted poster of Walter Pavlukoff. He told the police sergeant that he was sure it was the same man who had been in his store and whom he'd frequently seen in the area. He told the sergeant he'd keep an eye out, and when he saw the man a few weeks later, he called police.

Sergeant Arthur Varley and Constable John Bremner were sent to talk to the storekeeper and told to pick up the man that Moore pointed out to them. Pavlukoff insisted his name was Ralph McRae and that he was a carpenter who lived in the area. Varley told him that there had been complaints about a man hanging around there and he needed to come to the station to sort it out. Pavlukoff got in the police car and went quietly with them to the station.

He had done nothing to try to change his appearance and looked

---

17 Roddy Moore was murdered on October 17, 1947, and his story is part of *Cold Case Vancouver: The City's Most Baffling Unsolved Murders* (Arsenal Pulp Press, 2015).

Walter Pavlukoff. *Vancouver Province* March 28, 1953. *Courtesy of the Vance family*

just like his mug shot. When police searched him, Pavlukoff admitted his identity and told police, "I have nothing to hope for, and there is nothing I can say that will help me. I know they have a new rope waiting for me out there. I am glad it's all over."

The trial opened March 23, 1953, with a jury of ten men and two women. Pavlukoff appeared in court smartly dressed in a new double-breasted grey suit, white shirt, rust-coloured tie, and new brown shoes. He pleaded not guilty. Prosecutor Walter Owen read from the letters to Pavlukoff's mother that he had written from his Toronto rooming house the previous Christmas. "They want to hang me. I expect them to do so," read Owen. "I dread it."

In a newspaper clipping from the *Vancouver Sun* on January 26, 1953, Vance underlined several points in the story, including the first paragraph: "Mrs Ian MacGregor, attractive wife of a city police detective, in police court today identified Walter Pavlukoff as the holdup man. Two other witness had been unable to identify him at the hearing." Vance also underlined where he was mentioned as having received the Luger clip, the cartridge, the spent and damaged bullet, and the now moth-eaten hat with the initials W.P. At the trial, Vance acknowledged receipt of the pistol, but said that the notes he took in 1947 were missing from the lab. Without his notes, he could not positively state it was the same revolver, he said.

In the end it made little difference; it wouldn't have proven that Pavlukoff had fired the gun, just that the gun found on the beach had caused the death of Sydney Petrie. And while much of the evidence could have been explained away—such as the clothes and the hat with the initials W.P., even mistaken identification by the witnesses and the letters to his mother—finding the key to Pavlukoff's room was enough to convince the jury of his guilt. Judge Manson[18] passed the death sentence, the mandatory sentence for all murder convictions in Canada until 1962.

Pavlukoff's defence team immediately launched an appeal. The appeal failed, and Harold Fisher headed to Oakalla Prison Farm to tell his client in person. Pavlukoff returned to his prison cell on the second floor of the south wing while they prepared his cell on death row.

Pavlukoff had stolen a kitchen knife and then honed the blade on the concrete floor of his cell until it was razor-sharp. When the guard left, he stripped off his shirt, took the knife from its hiding place, stabbed himself in the heart, then threw himself face-down on the floor to make sure the blade killed him. The prison doctor reached Pavlukoff within minutes and desperately tried to bring him back to life so they could proceed to hang him. The doctor tried oxygen and stimulants, and when those failed, he made an incision in Pavlukoff's chest and massaged his damaged heart by hand. It was too late. Pavlukoff may have lost his trial and appeal, but in the end, he avoided the gallows and chose his own death.

---

18 In 1961, close to retirement, Manson—known as the "Hanging Judge" for his tendencies to favour the death penalty—said that the most sensational case of his twenty-six-year judicial career was the murder trial of Walter Pavlukoff. Manson, who'd sentenced fourteen convicted murderers to death, including Pavlukoff, said, "I never lost a night's sleep over any one of them."

EPILOGUE

On February 16 1949, an employment ad ran in the *Daily Province's* classified section under "Help Wanted." The job posting, for an analytical chemist for the city of Vancouver, was an attempt to find someone who could fill one of Vance's very large shoes. It read:

> City Analyst to perform chemical and physical analyses of a wide variety of foodstuffs, water samples, morgue specimens, explosives and other samples pertaining to public health and criminal investigation work. Qualifications: Master's degree in analytical chemistry or its equivalent in chemical and physical sciences. Extensive experience in chemical analyses. Preferably under age 40. Starting salary $357.50 per month.

Vance would turn sixty-five on May 2, 1949, the mandatory retirement age for a government position. Because he was owed some holidays, he told Chief Mulligan that his last day would be on April 6. The day before he was due to leave he'd given Chief Mulligan his badge and his Colt police revolver, which he'd had since 1932 on his appointment as Honorary Inspector. He returned his car to the city garage with a note thanking Maurice Baggs, the garage superintendent, for "the way in which you have kept this car in service under some of the most adverse conditions."

After he retired, Vance's workload was split in two. The Police Bureau of Science was renamed the Crime Detection Laboratory and headed up by police inspector Percy Easler, while Ted Fennell was appointed as the new city analyst. Fennell handled the chemical analysis and toxicology; Easler handled the physical science. The City Coroner Service became part of the provincial system in 1980. The morgue and autopsy facilities became part of Vancouver General Hospital. The city analyst's lab closed permanently in 1996 and all work was transferred to the RCMP crime laboratory.

During his four-decade-long career, Vance worked for thirteen police chiefs and sixteen mayors. L.D. Taylor, easily the most corrupt mayor and the one with whom Vance had the most trouble, is still the longest-serving mayor in Vancouver's history, in office for eleven non-consecutive years between 1910 and 1934. He died flat broke in 1946, aged eighty-eight. Gerry McGeer, the blustery lawyer who succeeded L.D. as mayor in 1934, died in August 1947, shortly after promoting Walter Mulligan to chief of police, the last chief to whom Vance would report.

Mulligan, who was the youngest chief in the history of the department, was also one of the most corrupt. By 1955, six years after Vance retired, Mulligan had 700 people under his command in a culture where cops routinely took bribes from bookies, bootleggers, and hardened criminals. That year, he was caught with his hand in the till. Things unravelled quickly when Detective Sergeant Len Cuthbert tried to kill himself with his service revolver but survived to testify at the Tupper Royal Commission into police corruption that he and Mulligan had doubled their salaries with bribes. Partway through the inquiry, Mulligan fled to California. Years later he returned to Canada, retired to the Victoria suburb of Oak Bay, and died in 1987.

Notorious brothel owner Joe Celona, who had been such good pals with Chief John Cameron in 1934, served eleven years in prison for conspiracy and was back in the news in 1955 when he was hauled in front of the Tupper Commission. He died three years later from colon cancer. Celona's death certificate says he was a divorced proprietor of a rooming house.

Detective Sergeant Percy Hoare, the hero of the False Creek Flats gun battle, retired from the police department almost two years to the day after the shootings and went to work in the security department of

BC Electric. In 1992, the eighty-five-year-old received a commendation from the VPD for courage in the line of fire. The shots that brought down two of the robbers at the False Creek flats hadn't been lucky ones; Hoare was one of a small group of police officers who started the Vancouver police shooters club and met once a week at the Stanley Park Armoury.

Vance reflects upon his 42-year career. *Daily Province,* April 7, 1949. *Courtesy of the Vance family*

William Faulder (Fats) Robertson, the seventeen-year-old who phoned in the anonymous tip to police the day of the False Creek Flats shootings, went on to enjoy a long career in crime and on the Vancouver Stock Exchange. In the early 1960s, Robertson made the headlines when he tried to turn the Wigwam Inn at Indian Arm, BC, into a gambling casino for millionaires. The police caught wind of it, and two boatloads of RCMP officers busted the old resort and uncovered an illegal gambling operation as well as plates for printing counterfeit money. Robertson and his partner Rockmill (Rocky) Myers, who unsuccessfully tried to bribe an RCMP officer, were convicted and sentenced to six years in prison. In 1972, Robertson lost his trading privileges on the Vancouver Stock Exchange for manipulating the share price of two junior mining companies. He was back in the headlines six years later when he was caught heading up a major drug smuggling ring. Police seized over $4 million worth of cocaine, and Robertson was again convicted and sentenced to prison, this time for twenty years.

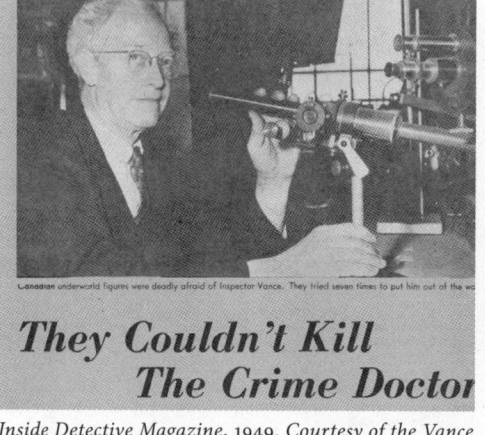

Canadian underworld figures were deadly afraid of Inspector Vance. They tried seven times to put him out of the wa

They Couldn't Kill
The Crime Docto

Inside Detective Magazine, 1949. Courtesy of the Vance family

Several key witnesses were given money to relocate and forge new identities. Robertson was released from prison after ten years and had his trading privileges reinstated. In 2003, he was back in the news yet again when a former insurance salesman from West Vancouver who moonlighted as a hit man said Robertson had contracted his services for two murders in 1969.

History books are full of stories about the bad and the colourful. Locally, there are books dedicated to the life and work of Vancouver's L.D. Taylor, Walter Mulligan, Gerry McGeer, and Angelo Branca. I've written on a few occasions about Joe Celona and former police chief John Cameron as well as the Lennie and Tupper Royal Commissions, two of the major inquiries into police corruption in the first half of the last century.

Good guys like J.F.C.B. Vance often seem to be unfairly passed over by history. Why isn't Vance more widely remembered for his amazing achievements and breakthroughs in forensic science?

As city analyst and head of the Police Bureau of Science, Vance went from obscurity in the 1920s to media celebrity, earning the moniker "The Sherlock Holmes of Canada," in the early '30s. He received a great deal of press, a lot of it spelled out in two-inch tall front-page headlines. By the middle of the decade, however, he seems to have faded back into obscurity for the remainder of his career.

There are likely a few reasons for this. Some criminals believed that

J.F.C.B. and Ethel Vance with their grandchildren, c.1950s. *Courtesy of the Vance family*

Vance's evidence alone could put them in jail, so they tried to stop him from testifying against them by attempting to murder or severely harm him. After several attempts on his life in 1934, his public profile was lowered, and he rarely appeared in the press unless he was giving evidence at trial. There were also few major developments in forensic science in the 1930s and 1940s. The American Academy of Forensic Sciences wasn't established until 1948, the year before Vance retired, and the first members were primarily from major US cities. DNA evidence, that game-changer for investigators, didn't come into play until 1987, when it was first used to solve a murder in England.

Doug Lucas, who started with the Centre of Forensic Sciences in Ontario in 1957 and retired as director four decades later, has a couple of theories about why Vance is not more widely remembered.

"I think that is a result of time and location. The only other forensic scientists in Canada were in Montreal and Toronto, and they didn't have much if any communication between them," he says. "There was only one journal that published papers on forensic science, and it was primarily devoted to criminology rather than forensic science." Lucas notes that Vance's counterpart in Toronto, Joslyn Rogers, Professor of Analytical Chemistry at the University of Toronto from 1914 to 1954, remained equally unknown outside of Ontario.

Kristin Hardie, former curator at the Vancouver Police Museum, says that Vance set up the framework for forensic science in Vancouver. "All of the framework that we have for investigators today are based on Vance's innovations and drive," she says. "Vance put a new fear of justice into criminals. Many crimes would have gone unsolved if Vance hadn't been there with his science."

After his retirement, the Vances sold their large Kerrisdale house and moved to the West End while they looked for a house "in the country." In 1950, Vance handed over all his research, dating back to 1927, for the "mechanical bloodhound"—the invention that had cemented his reputation as the Sherlock Holmes of Canada—to the British government.

The Vances eventually moved to a small house in South Surrey. Ethel Vance died in 1960 and John F.C.B. Vance four years later, at the age of eighty.

The Vancouver Police Museum has operated the building that housed Vance's lab since 1986.

February 21, 1949

Dr Stewart Murray,
Senior Medical Health Officer,
City Hall, 453 West 12th Ave.,
Vancouver, B.C.

Sir:

With reference to your telephone request for a list of
the examinations performed by this Laboratory, I beg to
submit the following things which this Division does for
various civic Departments:

Health Department
Food and drug analysis of every description
Beverage analysis
Milk analysis and milk product analysis
Water analysis, domestic and industrial
Examination of foreign substances in exhibits apart from
    official samples

Police Department
Identification and comparison of paints, soils, hair,
    stains, dust, glass, liquids and solids, etc.
Blood identification and grouping, human and animal
Identification of spermatozoa in suspected rape cases
Identification of gunpowder and other explosives
Identification of gun powder stains
Neutralization of explosives in safes, clothing and ma-
    terials
Liquor analysis, quantitative, also for drugs
Ballistics. Examination of weapons and ammunition
Comparison of footprints, tire tracks, etc.

Examination of altered or erased portions of documents

Examination of altered or erased serial numbers on radios, bicycles, autos, guns, etc.

Identification of marks on objects with the suspected tools which produced them

Examination of exhibits in abortion cases

Examination of clothing of suspected criminals

Analysis of metals, coal, ore, rock, soils, oil, asphalt, tar, cement, etc. in connection with crimes

Preparing and giving evidence in court trials on any of the above examinations and subject to cross examination by defence counsel

Coroner's Office

Examination of specimens from the human body, such as brain, blood, stomach and contents, bladder contents, liver, kidneys and heart, for poisons, drugs or liquor (quantitative analysis)

Examination of bodies, such as the hands and fingernails for evidence of powder, flesh, blood, fabric, hair, etc.; examination of skin for adhering substances; hair identification and comparison

Collection of blood and other specimens and material at scene of death

Examination of vomit collected near bodies

Engineering Department

Examination of water for dissolved minerals and for cause of corrosion of pipes and metals

Examination and identification of sewage and other substances

Fire Department

Identification of suspected incendiary materials

Determination of flash points of inflammable liquids

S.P.C.A.
Examination of suspected poison food, etc.
Examination of stomach contents, etc. of animals, birds
    and fowl, in suspected poisoning cases

Smoke Inspector
Examination of specimens collected to determine soot and
    dust accumulation

Vancouver General Hospital
Examination of stomach washings, etc. for poisons, drugs,
    etc. to determine treatment of patient
    undergoing emergency treatment
Examination of exhibits from bodies (intestinal organs
    and contents)

Purchasing Department
Examination of articles and materials for quality, re
    specifications

Parks Board
Soil analysis
Sea water analysis
Sea sand examination

In addition to the above there are examinations of
building materials for various departments.

Police Departments and Coroners from outside the City
of Vancouver request assistance in a variety of cases.
I have done these investigations at the request of the
Chief of Police, for which work no charge is made and no
fee received.

I am also frequently called out at night and on legal
holidays to examine accused persons and their clothing
for gunpowder, fabric, glass, hair, etc. in order that the

suspect may be released within the legal time he can be held without a charge being laid, for which no compensating time off is given.

Respectfully submitted,

John F.C.B. Vance
City, Provincial & Dominion Analyst
Chief Food & Dairy Inspector

...

BIBLIOGRAPHY

Books

Andersen, Earl. *Hard Place to Do Time: The Story of Oakalla Prison, 1912-1991*. New Westminster, BC: Hillpointe Publishing, 1993.

Bell, Suzanne. *Crime and Circumstance: Investigating the History of Forensic Science*. Westport, CT: Praeger, 2008.

Belshaw, John, ed. *Vancouver Confidential*. Vancouver: Anvil Press, 2014.

———, and Diane Purvey. *Vancouver Noir: 1930–1960*. Vancouver: Anvil Press, 2011.

Choy, Wayson. *All that Matters*. Toronto: Doubleday Canada, 2004.

Francis, Daniel. *Mayor Louis Taylor and the Rise of Vancouver*. Vancouver: Arsenal Pulp Press, 2004.

Ito, Roy. *Stories of My People: A Japanese Canadian Journal*. Hamilton, ON: S-20 and Nisei Veterans Association, 1994.

Kluckner, Michael. *Vanishing British Columbia*. Vancouver: University of British Columbia Press, 2005.

Lazarus, Eve. *At Home with History: The Untold Secrets of Greater Vancouver's Heritage Homes*. Vancouver: Anvil Press, 2007.

———. *Sensational Vancouver*. Vancouver: Anvil Press, 2014.

———. *Cold Case Vancouver: The City's Most Baffling Unsolved Murders*. Vancouver: Arsenal Pulp Press, 2015.

Lillard, Charles, and Robin Skelton. *The April Ghost of the Victoria Golf Links*. Victoria, BC: Hawthorne Society, 1994.

McDermid, Val. *Forensics: The Anatomy of Crime*. London, UK: Profile Books, 2014.

McDonald, Robert A.J., and Jean Barman, eds. *Vancouver Past: Essays in Social History*. Vancouver: University of British Columbia Press, 1986.

Macdonald, Ian, and Betty O'Keefe. *Dr. Fred and the Spanish Lady: Fighting the Killer Flu*. Surrey, BC: Heritage House Publishing, 2004.

Moore, Vincent. *Angelo Branca: Gladiator of the Courts.* Vancouver: Douglas and McIntyre, 1981.

Roy, Patricia. E. *A White Man's Province: British Columbia Politicians and Chinese and Japanese Immigrants, 1858-1914.* Vancouver: University of British Columbia Press, 1989.

———. *The Oriental Question: Consolidating a White Man's Province, 1914-1941.* Vancouver: University of British Columbia Press, 2003.

Sheehy, Elizabeth A. *Defending Battered Women on Trial: Lessons from the Transcripts.* Vancouver: University of British Columbia Press, 2014.

Yee, Paul. *Saltwater City: An Illustrated History of the Chinese in Vancouver.* Vancouver: Douglas and McIntyre, 2006.

Newspapers

The British Columbian
Daily Colonist
Daily Province
District News
Globe and Mail
Merritt Herald
Milwaukee Journal
Montreal Gazette
Nanaimo Free Press
North Vancouver Review
Ottawa Evening Journal
Spartanburg Herald
Spokesman Drummondville
Sydney Morning Herald
Toronto Star Weekly
Vancouver News Herald

Vancouver Star

Vancouver Sun

Victoria Daily Times

Victoria Times Colonist

The World

Journal Articles

Cameron, James D. "Canada's Struggle with Illegal Entry on Its West Coast: The Case of Fred Yoshy and Japanese Migrants before the Second World War." *BC Studies* 146 (Summer 2005): 37–62.

"Commemorating 75 years of Forensic Science in the RCMP." *The Quartet* (Spring 2013).

Huzel, James P. "Vancouver Past: The Incidence of Crime in Vancouver during the Great Depression." *BC Studies* 69–70 (Spring–Summer 1986): 211–48.

Lett, Stephen H. "Crime Detection Laboratory." *Scarlett & Gold* 68 (1987): 25–32.

———."The Regina Forensic Laboratory 50th Anniversary." *Scarlett & Gold* 69 (1988): 50–57.

Lucas, D.M. "CAC Founder's Lecture: The Development of Forensic Science in Canada." *Science & Justice* 37 no. 1 (1997): 47–54.

Prkachin, Yvan. "Chinks pay Heavily for Hitting Pipe: The Perception and Enforcement of Canada's New Drug Laws in Rural and Northern British Columbia, 1908-30." *BC Studies* 153 (Spring 2007): 73–105.

Sutherland, Neil. "The Triumph of 'Formalism,' Elementary Schooling in Vancouver from the 1920s to the 1960s." *BC Studies* 69-70 (Spring-Summer 1986): 175N210.

Tryhorn, F.G. "Scientific Aids in Criminal Investigation," *Police Journal* IX no. 1 (January–March 1936).

Canadian Police Gazette, November 1933.

National Home Monthly, September 1935.

Maclean's, November 1, 1934.

Standard Magazine, Montreal, August 20, 1949.

Other

City of Vancouver Archives, Map 191, 1907.

City Reflections, 1907, 2007. DVD. Vancouver Historical Society, 2008.

Vancouver Police Department Annual Reports (1907–49), Vancouver Police Museum.

Young, Michael G. *The History of Vancouver Youth Gangs: 1900–1985*. Unpublished M.A. thesis. Simon Fraser University, 1993.

ACKNOWLEDGMENTS

A ton of thanks goes to my friend Michael Kluckner who took on the first read of my unedited manuscript, sat me down in his kitchen, brewed coffee, made suggestions, corrected mistakes, and helped shape this into a much better book. A depth of gratitude also goes to Douglas M. Lucas, the former director of the Centre of Forensic Sciences in Ontario, and a man who probably knows more about the history of forensics than anyone on this planet. Doug kindly looked over my science, corrected, suggested, and tweaked. Credit for any mistakes that slipped through the cracks belongs solely to me.

I can't imagine *Blood, Sweat, and Fear* without the input of the Vance family. I was fortunate to meet with Marion Pocock, Vance's daughter, and her daughter Janey Johnson early in the process. Janey managed to unearth several boxes that belonged to J.F.C.B. Vance that contained documents, photos, notes, and memories. The information became integral to the story, and a lot of this material is featured in the book. Thank you also to David Vance, the genealogist in the family, who was able to supply much of the early history of the Vance family in Canada.

It would be impossible to write a book on true crime, forensics, or history without the help and resources of a number of people and institutions. Special thanks to Kristin Hardie and Rosslyn Shipp at the Vancouver Police Museum, to the staff at BC Archives who went out of their way to find long-lost records of inquests and preliminary hearings, to the staff at Vancouver Archives, the Vancouver Public Library's Special Collections, New Westminster Library, Linda Kawamoto Reid at the Nikkei National Museum, and Caroline Duncan at Oak Bay Archives.

I'd also like to thank the "Belshaw Gang," especially Tom Carter and Jason Vanderhill; Dr. Neil Boyd, professor of criminology at Simon Fraser University; Dr. Elizabeth Sheehy, professor of law at the University of Ottawa; Dr. David Klonsky, associate professor of psychology at the University of BC; and former Vancouver Police Department forensics specialist, Eric Grummisch for their time and expert assistance.

And, a huge thanks to the British Columbia Arts Council for awarding a grant for the writing of *Blood, Sweat, and Fear*.

I'm especially grateful to the amazing team at Arsenal Pulp Press. Thank you, Brian Lam, Robert Ballantyne, Cynara Geissler, Oliver McPartlin, and my exceptional editor, Susan Safyan.

INDEX

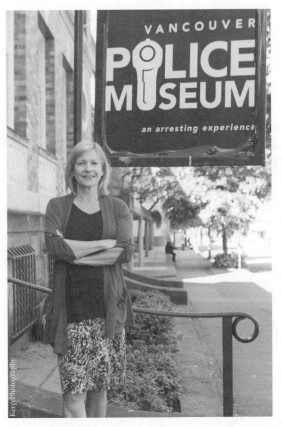

Eve Lazarus is a writer with a passion for non-traditional history and a fascination with murder. Her previous books include the BC bestsellers *Cold Case Vancouver: The City's Most Baffling Unsolved Murders* (Bill Duthie Booksellers' Choice Award finalist) and *Sensational Vancouver*. Eve lives in North Vancouver and blogs at *Every Place Has a Story*.

evelazarus.com